THE SHY MASTER

J.D. ERWYNN

ISBN 978-1-967508-97-6

Contents

Prologue

The only coherent thought racing through Gregory's mind as he lay sprawled on the cold cement floor was a single, desperate plea: **Help me.**

A metallic screech jolted him—a sharp, grating sound that echoed off the crumbling walls of the abandoned factory. The ax's blade dragged lazily along the hallway's edge with a sinister rhythm that looked like a countdown to his doom.

"Gregory!" The voice carried through the empty corridors, laced with a tone of mockery that sent a shiver down his spine.

Gregory tried to push himself upright, as his palms were scraping against the gritty floor, but his leg buckled beneath him. A bolt of searing pain shot up his calf, forcing him back down. Panting, he risked a glance at his injured leg and immediately regretted it. The gash was deep, the exposed flesh glistening in the moonlight as dark red blood pooled beneath him. The metallic scent filled the air, mingling with the factory's musty humidity.

He clenched his jaw. *I'm not going to die here. Not like this. Not by him.*

Tears blurred his vision, but he blinked them away. The primal fear in his chest was threatening to paralyze him, but he couldn't afford to freeze. *Think. Think.* His mind scrambled for a solution, but his thoughts dissolved into static every time the ax screeched closer.

"I just need to throw him off," he whispered, trembling. But how? With what?

The wind howled through the massive breaches in the walls, chilling his sweat-soaked skin. Gregory's breathing quickened as he clutched his leg, his blood-soaked hands trembling. He tried to staunch the flow, but the sticky warmth seeped between his fingers, leaving a vivid trail on the floor. A trail that the Mad Man was undoubtedly following.

"Gregoryyyy..." The voice came again, colder now, more deliberate. It bounced off the broken walls, making it impossible to pinpoint its source.

Gregory gritted his teeth and forced himself upright. His head spun, and his injured leg protested with every ounce of his weight, but he managed to steady himself against the wall.

The factory groaned around him with its skeletal structure straining against the harsh night wind. Rusted pipes hissed in the distance, as their corroded edges started dripping water that reeked of decay. Jagged shadows danced on the walls when moonlight filtered through the gaping holes in the ceiling, forming an eerie light on the debris-strewn floor.

He limped forward, silently praying for an exit, for salvation. His heart was pounding louder than the approaching footsteps, louder than the persistent screech of the ax. The corridor seemed an unbroken tunnel of darkness that swallowed him whole.

Then he stumbled. His hands shot out instinctively, catching a rusted beam before he hit the ground. The sharp edge tore into his palm, drawing blood, but he ignored it. Behind him, the footsteps slowed. He could feel the Mad Man's presence, oppressive and deliberate, as though savoring the hunt.

"Gregory." The voice was closer now, almost tender in its mockery. "Are we really going to play this game until the end?"

Gregory didn't respond. He bit his lip to stifle a groan as he pushed himself forward again. His leg burned with every step while his body was screaming at him to stop. He wouldn't. He couldn't.

But his strength was failing. He collapsed again, hitting his head on the floor with a dull thud. His vision swam as consciousness slipped away.

When Gregory opened his eyes, the Mad Man was there. The axe gleamed in the faint light, resting against the ground. Its polished edge, still smeared with Gregory's blood.

"Gregory, Gregory," the Mad Man crooned, circling him like a predator sizing up its prey. "This is disappointing. I expected more fight." He nudged Gregory's boot with his own, eliciting a weak flinch. "Still breathing? Good. I'd hate for this to end so soon."

Gregory's mind screamed at him to move, but his body refused. He was trapped with his strength spent, and his options gone. Tears slid silently down his cheeks as the Mad Man leaned closer, grinning.

"You had potential," the man whispered, breathing in the cold air. Then he straightened, hoisting the ax with both hands. "Too bad."

Gregory's eyes fluttered shut as the blade rose above him. He felt the shift in his surroundings.

And then—a sound. A faint scuffle behind them.

The Mad Man hesitated, snapping his head toward the noise. Gregory's eyes started to close as the Mad Man's shadow stood over him, and a wicked grin stretched across his face. The ax lifted high, catching a bit of moonlight as if teasing what was about to come. Tears rolled down Gregory's cheeks; he was too weak to fight back.

One chance. Just One.

The Mad Man shifted his stance, calm and confident, as if he had all the time in the world. Then, without a hint of hesitation, he swung.

Chapter One
Ethan

Ethan Bedford leaned heavily on the sticky bar counter. The overhead light was reflecting in his half-empty glass of bourbon. His surroundings smelled like spilled beer and despair, a fitting environment for a man like Ethan. He wasn't the kind of guy to start fights or cause a scene, but he was the kind who stayed too long, drank too much, and left just before the bartender could call him out on it.

"Another one?" the bartender asked, already reaching for the bottle.

Ethan nodded. "Might as well. Night's still young." He sounded dry, indifferent, as though he were discussing the weather rather than his steadily declining prospects in life.

"You're gonna end up with a breathalyzer strapped to your steering wheel, man," the bartender muttered, pouring the amber liquid.

Ethan smirked, lifting the glass. "Back roads and low beams. Works every time." He downed the drink in one smooth motion, ignoring the faint look of pity on the bartender's face. Conversations like this had played out countless times before. He knew what they were thinking: thirty years old, no stable job, no lasting relationships, just a guy slowly drinking himself into oblivion. Externally, he'd nod along, offering noncommittal agreements to deflect their concern. Internally, though, he sometimes wished things were different, just not enough to do anything about it.

The drive home was as predictable as the night itself. His ancient sedan creaked and groaned down the back roads, the headlights barely cutting through the dark. When he turned into his driveway, the house loomed like a forgotten relic. The pale blue paint had faded into a dull, sickly hue, and the porch light was, as always, conspicuously off.

Ethan fumbled with his keys, cursing under his breath when they slipped from his fingers. "Come on," he muttered, finally jamming the key into the lock on his third attempt. The door swung open, and he was greeted by the stale scent of beer and old takeout.

The living room was a graveyard of crushed cans and greasy wrappers. A sagging couch sat opposite a TV that hadn't been turned on in weeks. The walls bore scars from his worst moments—fist-sized holes he couldn't remember making. Some were patched up with clumsy swipes of plaster, their mismatched paint jobs standing out like wounds that had never quite healed.

Ethan shuffled through the mess, crunching his boots on something he didn't bother to identify. Nearly stumbled onto his kitchen counter. The instant smell of spoiled food and used dishes stacked poorly on top of one another. His hand leaned into an old, sticky spill of milk and cereal crumbs he had neglected to clean that morning. His commotion made the hum of dishes ring in his ears as his feet tried to find a solid foundation. Ethan's eyes strained in the darkness, staring at the bottle of booze toppled over. It felt like second nature to him to grapple the bottle and consume the poison. His stomach burned as he felt it run down, and yet it never dissuaded him from continuing to drink. Closing his eyes, relaxing to what he felt knew him most.

The hallway leading to his bedroom was dim, as the single bulb was flickering sporadically. His shoulder brushed the wall, and his gaze caught on the crooked frames of long-forgotten art pieces he'd picked up at a yard sale years ago. There were no family photos, no signs of a life shared with anyone else. Just empty spaces and half-hearted attempts at decoration.

By the time he reached his bedroom, exhaustion was clinging to him like a second skin. The door, perpetually open to avoid any more drunken collisions, swung slightly as he stumbled inside. He collapsed onto the unmade bed, the springs groaning in protest.

Ethan's head lolled to the side, catching the red glow of the alarm clock with his bleary eyes.

2:34 AM.

He sighed with the heavy sound of resignation. Morning was coming, and with it, another nine-to-five grind in the suffocating monotony of medical billing. The job paid enough to keep the lights on and the fridge semi-stocked, but it came with coworkers who insisted on small talk and office parties. The thought made his stomach turn. He especially dreaded Janice, his micromanaging supervisor with a penchant for condescension.

He then brushed his fingers at the edge of the nightstand, finding a half-full bottle of beer he didn't remember leaving there. He considered finishing it but set it back down, as his arm was too heavy to lift. Instead, he stared at the ceiling, letting the mild buzz in his head carry him closer to sleep.

As his breathing slowed, the sound of a car engine outside pulled him back from the edge of unconsciousness. It wasn't unusual for his neighbor to come home late, but something about the timing made him pause. He strained his ears as the sound faded into the distance. Shaking his head, Ethan dismissed it, finally closing his eyelids.

Tomorrow would come, whether he wanted it to or not.

BEEP. BEEP. BEEP.

The shrill cry of the alarm clock tore through the stillness of Ethan's room. He stirred, his body sluggish, as though his limbs were pulled down by invisible chains. His work uniform, wrinkled and stiff from yesterday's toil, clung to him. He rubbed his eyes, willing to make sense of the world.

The room was a battlefield of chaos with piles of discarded clothes spilling from chairs, an empty takeout box perched precariously on the edge of his desk, and a thin layer of dust on surfaces that hadn't been touched in weeks. Somewhere under it all, a sense of normalcy was buried, long forgotten.

Ethan swung his legs over the edge of the bed, deliberately moving. His feet met the cold floor as he shuffled to the bathroom with a foggy mind. The icy spray of the shower jolted him to life, reminding him of the day ahead.

Back in his room, he hunted through the clutter for a tie that wasn't too crumpled. The coffee pot in the corner of the kitchenette gurgled to life, filling the air with the bitter aroma of his one reliable solace. Ethan straightened his tie in the cracked mirror, its reflection warped, much like his mornings.

The coffee brewed in exactly five minutes—a fact Ethan knew not because he cared, but because of the breakroom encounters that had etched the timing into his memory. At work, those five minutes were a gauntlet. The breakroom, a space meant for reprieve, became a theater of absurdity where coworkers shared memes, traded jokes, and forced camaraderie he neither desired nor reciprocated.

The memory surfaced uninvited.

It had started like any other day. Ethan had walked into the breakroom, drawn by the need for caffeine more than conversation. But the atmosphere shifted the moment he entered. Eyes turned toward him—wide, expectant. He paused, uneasy.

"Ethan! Come here!" a voice chirped. Before he could react, a phone was thrust into his face.

On the screen, a video played. It showed him at his cubicle, oblivious to the fact that he'd been filmed. At first, he thought little of it. But then he saw the caption.

Looking for Pussy 21 & Older.

The room erupted in laughter.

He froze, scanning the array of emojis and comments scrolling below the video.

"He's hot!"

"Would totally screw him."

His face burned as a coworker read the comments aloud, mocking him. The room was filled with laughter ricocheting off the walls. Ethan's stomach churned. He'd never consented to this. To them, it was a joke. To him, it was a violation. He couldn't tell how miserable he felt that day. And the irony was that everything was happening in front of him. It felt like a slap in his face.

From that day forward, Ethan brewed his coffee at home. The quiet five minutes it took offered a rare preserve—a brief escape from the noise of the world.

As the coffee pot hissed its final note, he poured the brew into a battered thermos, grabbed his keys, and slung his laptop bag over his shoulder. The morning sun greeted him with an intensity he resented. Its rays cut through the neighborhood like a spotlight, illuminating everything he wished to avoid.

The neighbors were already out—chatting cheerfully, watering plants, walking dogs. Ethan kept his gaze low, hoping to evade the inevitable greetings. He made it to the car but paused, hearing a rustle in the bushes.

The small beagle emerged, wagging its tail furiously. The pup belonged to his elderly neighbor, who often forgot to secure the gate. Over the weeks, the dog had taken a liking to Ethan, and despite his cynicism, Ethan had grown fond of the creature.

Reaching into his pocket, he pulled out a crust of bread he'd saved from breakfast. The beagle took it eagerly, brushing its soft nose against his palm. Ethan patted its head lightly, watching as it scampered off.

Sliding into the driver's seat of his gray 2003 Nissan Altima, he sighed. The car was as tired as he was. Its interior was littered with beer cans and fast-food wrappers. He turned the ignition, the engine sputtering before coming to life.

As he pulled out of the driveway, the sun glared through the windshield, forcing him to squint. Another day awaited with a string of conversations he didn't want to have; with people he'd rather avoid. But as the beagle disappeared into the bushes, a spark of something— call it hope, or maybe just habit—kept him moving forward.

The road stretched ahead, indifferent to his thoughts. For Ethan, it was both a curse and a source of respite.

Ethan exhaled slowly, as the thrum of his pulse gradually subsided. He leaned back in the driver's seat. The tinted windows cloaked him in privacy, blocking him and the curious eyes of the world outside.

From his shirt pocket, he retrieved a crumpled cigarette pack. Pulling one out, he lit it with a practiced flick of his lighter. The flame illuminated the faint tremor in his hand before disappearing. He didn't roll down the windows. The smoke was swirling around him, and its acrid scent was mixing with the aroma of old upholstery. The familiar sting in his throat was oddly grounding.

For a moment, he stared at the steering wheel, letting the haze settle. Then, without ceremony, he turned the ignition. The engine hummed to life, steady and reliable, contrasting with the noise that awaited him later.

The drive to work offered a rare reprieve. Early morning sunlight streaked the buildings, forming fleeting shadows across his windshield. Traffic was mercifully light; the radio was playing slowly in the background. This was the part of his day Ethan almost looked forward to—the calm before the storm.

When he reached the bar, the morning rush was in full swing. Ethan's office was tucked away on the third floor, a lit sanctuary where he could retreat from the chaos below. His coffee, already drained during the drive, left him craving more. He headed straight to the break room to be greeted by the coffee pot's gurgle. He was grateful no one else was there. Small talk before caffeine was unthinkable.

He poured a fresh cup, watching the dark liquid swirl into the mug. The heat seeped through the ceramic, warming his hands as his thoughts drifted. What would today bring? Another moment to endure? Another situation to navigate with gritted teeth? He sighed, taking his first sip, when—

TAP. TAP.

Ethan froze, cup halfway to his lips. He didn't need to look up to know who it was. The sharp and impatient beat of the knock was unmistakable.

Terry Orville.

Terry leaned against the doorframe with a sharp grin in his tailored suit. The scent of cheap cologne preceded him, mingling with the lingering coffee aroma. Terry's hair, greying at the temples, was swept back with meticulous care, but the disheveled collar betrayed his morning's escapades.

"You look like you've seen a ghost," Terry quipped, stepping inside and glancing over his shoulder to ensure they were alone.

Ethan blew on his coffee, curling his lips into a faint smirk. "And you look like you survived one."

Terry frowned, tugging at his collar. Red scratches and faint bruises peeked out, poorly concealed by the crisp white fabric. With a sheepish laugh, he adjusted his tie, hiding the evidence more effectively.

"She's a handful, you know that," Terry admitted, running a hand through his hair.

"Sure," Ethan murmured.

Terry laughed, echoing in the small room. With a conspiratorial wink, he headed for the door. "Don't work too hard."

Ethan watched him leave, swinging the break room door shut behind him. He sipped his coffee, savoring the quiet moment before returning to his desk. Terry's presence, as usual, was in equal parts irritating and oddly reassuring.

Ethan couldn't help but think back to the one moment that made him respect Terry, no matter how grating the man's personality could sometimes be. It had been during a team meeting—one of those unbearable sessions where Janice loved to show off her authority.

Ethan had felt the familiar panic, his shallow breathing and trembling hands. The anxiety built up so quickly he couldn't stop it, and before he knew it, he had thrown up right there on the conference table. The room went silent except for the sound of his chair scraping back as he tried to clean himself up. Janice, of course, wasted no time tearing into him.

"Honestly, Bedford, can't you pull yourself together?" she snapped in a tone laced with condescension. Ethan had been too mortified to respond, but Terry had slammed his hands on the table with a booming voice that cut through the tension. "Back off, Janice. He's clearly going through something, and you're making it worse!" The room froze, Janice turning beet red as Terry glared her down. She didn't say another word about it, and the meeting quickly moved on, but the memory stuck with Ethan. Terry might've been loud and obnoxious at times, but at least he was human—and that was more than Ethan could say for most people in that office.

The day crawled forward, punctuated by the clatter of keyboards and the occasional conversation. Terry, seated across from Ethan, worked in uncharacteristic silence. Ethan appreciated that about him. Despite his flamboyant personality, Terry knew when to keep his head down.

As the clock ticked closer to quitting time, Ethan began to gather his things with an efficiency born of desperation. He double-checked his desk, ensuring there was nothing to warrant a return. The haze of the cigarette he'd light in his car beckoned, a promise of solitude to end the day.

By the time he stepped outside, the sun had painted the sky in muted tones. Ethan slid into his car, hiding behind the tinted windows that once again shielded him from the world. He lit another cigarette, which illuminated his face before fading into the encroaching darkness.

Tomorrow would come, as it always did. But for now, he had this—a fleeting moment of peace, suspended between the chaos of today and the uncertainty of what lay ahead.

Chapter Two
Card

Ethan was back at the same bar, perched on the same worn stool, surrounded by the same veil of lighting and stale air. The smell of spilled beer and faint cologne remained in the cracks of the wooden counter. The bartender, a man of few words, slid over Ethan's third beer without a question. This was his routine as predictable as Ethan's own.

Ethan stared at the amber liquid, grounded in the moment. The muffled chatter of the crowd behind him ebbed and flowed, and a tide of indistinct voices blended with the occasional clink of glassware. The haze was settling in. This was his escape, his ritual, his oblivion.

The scrape of a stool against the floor sliced through the background noise. A man sat down beside him, his movements were precise and unhurried. Ethan glanced over, his curiosity piqued despite himself. The man's appearance was striking—a perfectly tailored black suit hugged his frame, every seam impeccable. His diamond-studded earrings glimmered each time they caught the light, an odd flourish for a place like this.

"Gin and tonic," the man ordered in a crisp and self-assuring voice.

The bartender nodded silently and began pouring. Ethan's gaze stayed, full of intrigue and unease bubbling beneath the surface. What was a man like him doing here? The man turned slightly, catching Ethan's persistent stare. His lips curled into a faint smirk.

"Can I help you?" he asked, lightly, but it seemed he was pointing at something.

Ethan's eyes darted back to his drink with embarrassment pricking his skin. "Sorry," he muttered, unsure why his attention had fixated so intently on the stranger.

"It's the suit, isn't it?" The man leaned back slightly, widening his grin as he gestured at himself.

Ethan remained silent, unwilling to confirm the observation. He wasn't sure if it was the suit, the air of confidence, or something else entirely that held his attention.

The man chuckled softly. "Don't worry, Ethan, it happens all the time."

Ethan stared at the man, his expression shifting to one of utter bewilderment.

"It is Ethan, right?" Asked the man, extending his hand across the narrow space between them. "I'm Sebastian."

Ethan hesitated, staring at the outstretched hand. His confusion deepened. "Sebastian?" he repeated in a voice edged with suspicion. "How do you know my name?"

The smirk faltered for a fraction of a second before returning with practiced ease. Sebastian let his hand fall. "I have a knack for reading people," he said cryptically. "You always seem stressed. Tough job?"

Ethan's grip tightened around his glass. Anger stirred in the pit of his stomach. "Who are you?" he asked, his voice taut with restrained frustration.

"A potential friend." Sebastian's tone was calm, unbothered. He reached into his jacket pocket and pulled out a sleek business card, sliding it across the counter toward Ethan.

Ethan glanced at the card, furrowing his brows as he read the elegant print.

"Dr. Elijah Tatler Fear Doctor"

The words seemed absurd, almost laughable. Ethan let out a dry, disbelieving chuckle. "Fear doctor?" he said, almost choking on his beer. "What happened to therapists?"

Sebastian didn't miss a beat. "Call him what you want. He's the best in the business," he said, lifting his glass to his lips. The bartender placed Sebastian's drink in front of him, clinking the ice softly.

"I don't need therapy," Ethan replied in a sharper voice than before. "And I'm not afraid of anything."

Sebastian tilted his head, studying him with an almost amused expression. "Is that right?" he asked, skeptical. "Everyone's afraid of something, Ethan. Scars don't always show on the surface."

Ethan shifted uncomfortably on his stool. The words hit closer to home than he wanted to admit. He stared at his empty glass, refusing to meet Sebastian's gaze. The man's presence was unnerving, and his insights were uncomfortably accurate for someone who was supposedly a stranger.

"So, what's his deal? This Dr. Tatler?" Ethan finally asked casually but failed to mask his curiosity.

Sebastian's smile widened. "Let's just say he helps you face your fears. Really face them. And when you do, it's like a burden lifts, like butterflies in your stomach." His voice took on a faintly reverent tone. "I used to be afraid of almost everything. Now, there's nothing in this world that scares me."

Sebastian drained the last of his drink, pulled a stack of neatly folded bills from his pocket, and placed them under his glass. He stood, smoothing his suit with practiced precision. "You should think about it," he said, dropping his voice to a near-whisper.

Ethan frowned. "How do you know my name?" he asked again, but barely audible this time.

Sebastian's smirk returned, tinged with something darker, more elusive. He clapped Ethan on the back as he turned to leave. "See you around, Ethan."

And just like that, he was gone, leaving Ethan alone with his thoughts, a business card, and the faintest chill in the air.

Three days had crawled by, and Ethan's mind hadn't let go of the card. The name *Sebastian* stayed like a question he couldn't answer, tethered to the strange encounter that refused to fade. Each time he rifled through his bag, his fingers found the small card, pulling it out almost reflexively. He would stare at the number, hovering over the keypad with his thumb.

What held him back? Was it fear of the unknown? Or perhaps an inherent distrust of solutions that seemed too good to be true?

The thought gnawed at him. If he called and it turned out to be legitimate, what then? Was he ready for whatever *cure* this mysterious Dr. Tatler offered? And what if it was a scam—a predatory setup designed to exploit people desperate for answers? He didn't want to be another gullible victim.

Setting the card aside, Ethan tapped the *Enter* key twice to wake his computer. His fingers hesitated above the keyboard before typing "Dr. Tatler" into the search bar, followed by the office address Sebastian had mentioned. The results loaded sluggishly, as if sharing Ethan's reluctance.

The search revealed a vague description of an office and a flood of glowing reviews from former patients. Five stars across the board, with effusive praise for the *phenomenal work* Dr. Tatler had done. Yet not a single image of the man himself. Ethan scrolled and scrolled, frowning as page after page came up empty.

"Odd," he murmured, leaning back in his chair.

He tried to rationalize it. Some people hated being photographed. Ethan understood that well enough. He avoided cameras like the plague. Having a lens pointed at him felt like being under a microscope, every flaw magnified. He loathed being the center of attention, and maybe Dr. Tatler was the same.

Still, something about it unsettled him. The cursor blinked impatiently on the screen as Ethan ran a hand over his face.

The sharp slap of a paper stack landing on his desk startled him. His stomach twisted as he looked up to see Janice looming over him, her posture rigid and domineering. She was so close he could smell her—the cloying blend of oatmeal cookies and cheap floral perfume that always made his head spin.

"Ethan, why aren't you working?" Her voice was saccharine, but her sharp tone betrayed her frustration. She popped a piece of gum into her mouth, chewing noisily as she stared him down.

Ethan's palms began to sweat. Of all the people in the office, Janice was the only one who could unravel him so completely.

"I need you to make calls. *Now!*" Her voice rose, loud enough to draw the attention of their coworkers. Heads turned, and Ethan felt the familiar weight of their stares.

His chest tightened. Janice's presence always triggered something visceral in him—a memory of another voice, another figure standing over him, yelling with the same venom. His mother. The mental image surfaced unbidden: her face close to his, spittle flying as she screamed. The vibrations of her voice still rang in his ears years later.

He reached for the phone, his fingers trembling. Dialing felt like an Olympic feat, and the first ring sent his pulse racing. By the second, he was lightheaded. A calm voice finally answered, but his tongue felt heavy, stuck to the roof of his mouth.

"Hello?" the voice said again, more insistent this time.

Janice leaned in, her impatience palpable. "Speak!" she hissed, her arms crossed like a disappointed teacher.

Ethan's mind went blank. He stared at the phone as the voice on the other end repeated their greeting. His silence stretched, unbearable. Finally, the call disconnected with a hollow beep.

"They hung up," he managed weakly, his voice barely audible.

Janice rolled her eyes, snatching the receiver. "Unbelievable. I guess I have to do *everything* myself." She dialed the number again, this time putting the call on speaker. The office went eerily quiet, every face trained on Ethan.

"I have to train you like a toddler, obviously," she muttered, her voice dripping with disdain.

The phone rang, and Ethan's body trembled with dread. When the voice answered again, the pressure became unbearable. He bolted upright, nearly knocking Janice over as he grabbed his bag and made a beeline for the elevator.

"Ethan!" she called after him, but he didn't turn back. He didn't care. He needed to escape. The elevator doors couldn't open fast enough.

Once outside, the cold air hit him like a slap. He wandered aimlessly until he found himself at his usual haunt. The bar was dimly lit and sparsely populated—just the way he liked it.

Four drinks in, Ethan's thoughts were swimming in the same loop. The confrontation with Janice replayed in his mind, each detail vivid and unforgiving. He thought about what he *should* have said, the words he'd swallowed that now burned in his throat.

Reaching into his pocket, he pulled out the card. It was crumpled, the edges soft from handling. His gaze drifted to the empty stool where Sebastian had sat three nights ago.

Ethan let out a long sigh and pulled out his phone. For a moment, he stared at the screen, hesitating. Then, with a deep breath, he dialed the number.

The line rang once. Twice.

And then, a voice answered.

$\smile\!\!\infty$

Chapter Three
Doctor Tatler

Ethan sat outside the office. The building was small, with a brown and charcoal brick pattern. The only car in the parking lot besides Ethan's was a brand-new black Cadillac with blacked-out windows. Must be the doctor's—what other person could afford it?

Ethan got out of his car, looking around the empty parking lot. At the door, the name read "Dr. Elijah Tatler." A little odd that it didn't specify he was a therapist. Ethan pulled the door open.

The place was clean and organized. At the large desk at the end of the room sat a woman in a white dress that fit her figure perfectly, not tight, yet not too loose. Her dark hair was pulled back in the neatest bun he had ever seen. Her skin was pale, and her crimson lipstick made her appear more daunting. Ethan's entrance didn't shift her; she continued to type on her computer as if he'd never entered the room. Maybe she was busy confirming another appointment, but she hadn't batted an eye toward him.

Ethan grazed his thumb along the edge of the counter. "Hello, ah, I'm Ethan. I scheduled an appointment with Dr. Tatler."

The woman continued to type. He knew she heard him so much for customer service.

"Ma'am?" Ethan's voice sounded more agitated.

The typing abruptly stopped.

"Ethan Bedford. Your appointment is confirmed." She resumed her typing, minding nobody but her own business.

"How long until he sees me?" Ethan maintained his composure.

The woman did not blink at his words. He decided to take a seat, occasionally eyeing the woman in white. Slight murmuring came from the door at the end of the hallway—Ethan hadn't noticed it before. An image passed by it, then two.

Great, he thought. They're finishing up.

He leaned forward, wiping his palms onto his jeans. He rummaged through his thoughts. What was he doing there? The still calmness made him more anxious, always expecting it to be disturbed by her disturbance of peace. His mouth was filling with the familiar salty taste, followed by the ringing in his ears from the yells she— Stop.

Ethan had to stop thinking of her. The door opened. Thank god. A man emerged, young, maybe a little younger than Ethan. His demeanor was quaint. The light murmur Ethan had heard in the room sounded upbeat, yet the man kept his head low, intentionally avoiding eye contact as he scurried past. Ethan stood, ready for his name to be called. The door remained cracked open. Ethan glanced once more at the Woman in White.

Maybe she was the one to tell him when it was time to go in. But no, she typed on. A beep sounded along with a bright red light placed above the door.

"The Doctor will see you now." The woman in white stood motionless in front of the desk she'd been behind a second ago, her eyes hollow. Ethan was taken aback. How had she managed to move so fast, without any commotion?

Her face was cold, and her stare unmoving. The ends of her dress dangled around her ankles, slightly covering her vintage Oxford shoes. Ethan cautiously walked to the room with the red light. He knocked warily on the door, causing it to push open further.

A voice broke out. "Come in."

Ethan gently pushed the door all the way open. A tall man was placing a book on the shelf, his back turned. He wore a white dress shirt; his black slacks matched him well. He wore a clean pair of black oxfords that clicked whenever he stepped. The most distinct thing about him was what was on his head—a top hat.

Ethan snickered at the sight of it. Maybe the doctor had a unique fashion sense.

The room was typical. The walls were a gentle taupe color, simple, like he'd watched on TV. It had one comfy chair meant for the doctor; a small couch sat opposite it with a coffee table between. Neatly placed magazines for bored patients and a bowl of hard candied mints in green wrappers decorated the table. Ethan's eyes were drawn to the vintage record player. A gentle tune played lowly as he corrected his footing in front of the couch.

Ethan sat, trying his best to get comfortable for a session that could go well or up in flames.

Doctor Tatler broke the silence. "Ethan Bedford."

He finally turned around, revealing a man with a wide grin. His wrinkles straightened out as his smile expanded. Under his hat, Ethan could tell his hair had been a deep brown in his youth, now more grey than anything.

He grabbed a clipboard and sat in the chair across from Ethan. Ethan rubbed his hands together, feeling odd about not knowing what the doctor would ask, or if he'd immediately diagnose him with an illness he never knew existed.

"Ethan Bedford. How are you today?" The doctor leaned back, his voice soothing.

"I'm fine." Ethan looked down at the bowl of green mints. Did the doctor make him so nervous that he couldn't ask for a candy?

"Would you like one?" The doctor picked up the bowl and showed it to Ethan. Not typical mints—these were square-shaped, and the wrapper looked as if someone had poorly twisted it together. Still, Ethan took one. Maybe the peppermint would calm his nerves.

He opened the mint and swallowed. It was strong, barely tasting of mint at all. And chalky.

Still, not wanting to offend, he swallowed.

"These are mints, right?" Ethan gave a small chuckle.

Doctor Tatler smiled, smiled just like the woman in white. His face was slowly grimacing.

"So, what are you in here for?" He tapped his pen on the clipboard.

"Honestly, I don't know why. Sebastian referred me." Ethan took a deep breath.

Tatler grimaced again. Ethan hadn't noticed as he continued to speak.

"I've been overwhelmed. Work. Life." Ethan looked down.

"Go on, Mr. Bedford."

An hour passed, and Ethan was finishing up. He couldn't believe how light he felt from talking. Doctor Tatler listened and wrote. When he spoke, it was to ask Ethan about what bothered him: his job, Janice, his drinking. He asked twice about Ethan's childhood, which Ethan quickly glossed over.

Doctor Tatler scribbled a final note. "Thank you, Ethan. You gave us great insight."

Us? Maybe he misspoke.

The doctor stood, correcting his pants from being creased so long from sitting. Ethan pressed himself up and just as quickly fell back down. His eyes felt heavy.

"Are you alright, Mr. Bedford?" Doctor Tatler pressed his hand to his head. Sweat began to fall on his cheek. Ethan wasn't responding.

Paramedics, Ethan thought. His mouth couldn't open, yet something was wrong, and what he needed was help.

Doctor Tatler propped Ethan up, gently caressing his cheek once more before he faded, and Ethan heard one thing:

"It'll... be... alright."

Chapter Four
Fear

BEEP BEEP BEEP

Ethan shot up. He was lying in his bed, in his room, in his house. Confusion began to wash over his face as he tried to piece together what happened after he left Doctor Tatler's office.

But he couldn't. He couldn't remember saying goodbye to Doctor Tatler or the woman in white, starting his car, or stumbling into his bed. Everything was a blur.

Ethan looked down and saw his body bare. He never slept naked. He might've thought that was something he could've done himself, but he couldn't have—he'd stayed sober that day for Doctor Tatler. Never once had he come home in his drunken stupor and undressed himself completely. Ethan felt the old bruises around his stomach. His gut felt nauseous as he ran his fingers over the marks, wounds that never healed. Checking his alarm clock, he saw it was time to prepare for work.

After throwing on whatever he could find and making his morning coffee, he swung open the door and headed for his car. He heard faint yelps as the pup ran up to him. That was his cue as he pulled the bread from his pocket and set it on the ground. The pup devoured it in three bites and scurried off.

The elevator doors opened, and Ethan rushed out. His coffee spilled over his hands—he'd been so thrown this morning he hadn't corrected the lid until he arrived at work. Everyone gave short glances, trying to tell if he was still shaken from Janice the day before. Ethan kept his gaze on his desk, praying no one would ask how he was.

Thankfully, he made it, leaning back in his chair and swaying back and forth, reflecting on what happened.

Why can't I remember?

Maybe he did make it to the bar first, so buoyantly proud of his session, he took it farther than usual. Ethan pulled out his phone and dialed the doctor's number. No answer. His office should be open. Regardless, his office was on Ethan's way home, and he could talk to him then.

"Knock, knock." Terry leaned in. I'm sure word of Janice's belittlement had spread around. Ethan wasn't willing to express, although he wanted to vaguely tell Terry it happened and how he wanted to move on.

Luckily, Terry was good at reading facial cues. One look at Ethan, and he knew Ethan didn't want to be bothered. So Terry faced his desk and worked.

The day dragged. Ethan eyed down the last hour, finally hitting five o'clock. Bolting for the elevator door, then to his car.

Arriving at Dr. Tatler's, the parking lot was empty again except for that same black car. Ethan entered the office. No one was there, not even the Woman in White. Ethan wasn't too surprised, considering the service he'd received from her the day before.

Heading toward Dr. Tatler's office, he pressed the door softly in case he was already in session. Dr. Tatler sat in his chair, writing on the clipboard. Ethan barely saw his face as that ridiculous top hat blocked his view.

"Ethan?" Tatler said while not finishing his sentence on the clipboard.

He walked in and sat.

"You're here early."

Ethan nodded in agreement.

"I didn't see your receptionist." Ethan wiped his hands.

Dr. Tatler smiled, gently clicking the top of his pen.

"I'm so glad you're back, Ethan." Ethan forced a smirk. He was happy to feel heard, yet when he entered the office, he clammed up like his young self.

Dr. Tatler asked the simple questions: How was your day? How do you feel? Are you okay?

Ethan replied with simple answers: Fine. Okay. Yes.

Dr. Tatler wrote and wrote.

Periodically looking up, as he could feel Ethan's sense of unease. Tatler shook his hand, motioning for Ethan to stop. Ethan sat back, rubbing his neck, knowing the question Tatler would ask.

"What's wrong, Ethan? Something's bothering you?" Tatler crossed his legs and leaned back. Taking heed, as Ethan cleared his throat, recollecting the shameful event of Janice demeaning him a day ago, his body calming as he delineated.

"Janice makes me sick, the way she treats me." Ethan clenched his fist, envisioning that she was right in front of him. He could punch a hole right through her from the wrath he suppressed. Tatler remained still, seeing the venom Ethan was wishing on Janice.

"You feel as if Janice could die and you'd be alright?" Tatler stated, jotting on his clipboard again. Ethan looked up in confusion. He didn't want the Doctor to think he was a psycho, but he had no love for Janice.

"What?! No. Janice is a difficult person, but I just want her to go away." Ethan's eyes pleaded as he hung his head low.

"Some days I wonder if she'll have a heart attack." Ethan felt the instant need to redact that statement, although that's how he felt. Janice was a problem in his life. A problem he knew wasn't going away. For a moment, Ethan could've sworn he saw Tatler smirk.

The session was coming to a close. Yet again, he oddly felt relieved.

"What did your mother do to you, Ethan?" Ethan looked frazzled. What a random question when everything was going so well. How did he know what happened between him and his mother?

"Excuse me?" Ethan looked uncomfortable. His body retreated into itself. He felt the mention of his mother was going to make him ill.

Ethan leaned forward and grabbed a mint, popping it into his mouth so fast he almost forgot the chalky taste.

Dr. Tatler tapped his pen. "How can you beat your fear if you don't confront it?"

Ethan was taken aback now. "My fear? I'm not afraid."

Dr. Tatler looked serious, like what Ethan said wasn't a joke. He stared cold. Alright, this was a little too much.

"Ethan, what did she do?" Dr. Tatler was still, and his face went from cheerful to stern.

Ethan stood up, his face furious. "I told you, I don't want to talk about that!" Ethan quickly came to a realization. Why fight?

Ethan dug his fingers into his pants, trying hard not to stutter. "I—" He forced the sentence out. "I want to leave!"

Doctor Tatler didn't break his intimidating gaze.

Ethan grabbed the doorknob.

"Ethan, sit," Doctor Tatler commanded.

Ethan, now furious, turned the knob to startlement. The Woman in White stood motionless. Her smile was wicked.

"Move!" Ethan shouted, but the Woman in White still stood. Ethan turned around to find Dr. Tatler closer than he'd ever been.

"Ethan, our session isn't over." Dr. Tatler grimaced. "I'm here to help you. Help you feel the butterflies in your stomach."

Ethan felt faint again. His body began to feel heavy as Dr. Tatler went on. "Ethan, how can I help you with the trauma of your mother if you don't allow me to?"

Ethan pushed Dr. Tatler. The force barely affected him. The woman grabbed the statue from the corner of the room, hitting it on Ethan's head. The thud knocked Ethan back. His strength was depleting, and he could possibly be in the arms of two bizarre individuals.

"Let me—"

Ethan collapsed into Dr. Tatler's arms.

***

Ethan awoke, shooting up in the darkness. Leaning over to check the time.

3:17 A.M.

Ethan rubbed his face. The pain surged in the back of his head. Reaching back, his hand was covered in dried blood. He looked around, thinking of the doctor and his creepy mistress.

Bastards.

Ethan pulled his covers off, sliding off his bed. His body still had the heaviness of how he felt before. Slowly shuffling to the kitchen, he grabbed a glass from the cabinet and filled it with water from the sink that wasn't filled with dishes. Lifting the glass to his lips, he looked straight ahead to his bedroom. The door was wide open, and in it stood a silhouette of a woman—the Woman in White's silhouette.

Ethan froze. Cornering him at the office was one thing, but for her to be in his home? The figure stood still as Ethan slowly placed his drink on the countertop.

His eyes shifted toward the knife holder. If she was making a move, so was he. Creeping slowly toward the knives, Ethan's heart began to race. What should he do? Call out to the stranger? Make a run for the door? Ethan was a few inches away as the figure walked back and slammed his bedroom door shut.

Ethan nearly reached for the knife, cut off by a forceful push into the counter. His side stung, and he gasped for air, clenching his ribcage.

The figure lifted Ethan up, slamming his head into the sink. Inhaling the liquid made his throat burn. The figure lifted his head up, allowing a breath of air. The taste was a mixture of alcohol—beer, whiskey, and Ethan tasted it all as the figure pressed his head down again, more forceful than last time. Ethan's only thought was that he was going to die, die in the ocean of what he cared about most. Irony.

Ethan was fading, and the darkness was pulling him into the memory of what he was trying to hide the most.

***

Ethan's head lifted up. His mother had done it again, like she always did, calling him Darren and saying how upset he made that her for not picked up his toys that he had promised to do earlier.

Ethan cried as his body lay on the wet floor. His mother marched off to her room, slamming the door. It was always about Darren.

Darren was Ethan's father, who left them when Ethan was seven—that was three years ago. Ethan often questioned why leave him? With her?

Ethan sat for about twenty minutes. When his mother acted this way, she would retreat into her room for the rest of the day, refusing to answer for anything. If he was hungry, he had to learn to find something that didn't need to be cooked. If he was sick, he had to pray the fever would leave as quickly as it came. So, since he knew he had the evening to himself, he cleaned and hoped her angst went away as quickly as the fever.

***

Ethan pressed his head up with all his strength. He still couldn't see, and the alcohol still burned his lungs. Feeling around for anything, he felt the fleshy—

Flesh!

Ethan scratched harder than he had ever scratched in his life. The figure let go, and Ethan could breathe again. He coughed and coughed, wiping away the booze from his eyes. Turning around to no one. The house was quiet again. He ran toward the front door. His keys hung on the hook next to the peephole. Ethan swiped the keys and sprinted for his car, pulling out onto the road as the figure watched him through the window.

Chapter Five
One Week

Two days had passed since Ethan had seen the figure in the hallway. He felt less anxious when the police entered and searched. They found nothing. By the time Ethan and the police came back, everything had been cleaned up. His house was spotless. The strong odor of the booze-filled sink had dissipated, and the small drips of blood left by the intruder were washed away. His heart sank. And now, Ethan had grown weary of being considered crazy.

Who was that figure? It couldn't have been that woman. Ethan had only met them twice and had never given them any information. They never asked him to fill out any paperwork.

Ethan recounted the Woman in White's opening words ringing in his ears: "Ethan Bedford, your appointment is confirmed."

He never gave her his last name. He felt his vision constrict. What had he done?

The police did little to calm Ethan's fears. They told him they'd check in on it, exchanging confused looks before leaving. His mind was too jaded. Luckily, the weekend hit and Ethan could have one less thing to worry about. He couldn't stay in that house alone, especially at night.

He decided to go on a drive. Anything to not feel trapped in that house. Ethan drove and drove until he arrived at the office. The parking lot was empty yet again. Cautiously, Ethan entered, making his way through the lobby. No one was in sight. He looked at the door at the end of the hallway. The light was on, and a shadow reflected off the bottom of the door. Ethan, discreet yet fierce, trudged his way to the room. There sat Tatler in his chair, as if nothing had happened.

"You drugged me!" Ethan's face began to turn red. His anger was festering.

Tatler remained calm. He gently set his notepad on the table and asked, "Ethan, I have no idea what you're talking about."

Ethan's face grew red again. He wasn't crazy; that had to have happened.

Tatler remained composed. "Are you sure it wasn't a dream, Mr. Bedford?" He tried to explain that patients are not far from having episodic delusions, especially if a family member conveys it.

Ethan's body began to fill with rage, a rage he hadn't felt in a long time. His hands curled, and his stance grew wide as he shouted, "Where's your assistant? Huh?!"

"She's been sick the last few days," Tatler said with so much repose.

Ethan calmed—maybe he did dream it all. But it was so real. The bruises were still on his side. The pain from it spiked when he moved too quickly or spoke too loud. Ethan looked over the empty corner of the room, the empty spot where the statue was before. Staring at the spot made his head hurt again. His memory blurred as a piece of him was flooding back... His body felt like it was losing all control as he collapsed into Tatler's arms, setting him gently on the couch. Tatler adjusted Ethan's head as the Woman in White set the bloodied statue on the coffee table. Ethan's mind wanted to reach for it, but his body wouldn't follow his desire. He slowly blinked in and out of consciousness as Tatler leaned back in his chair, biting his fingers, snickering to himself.

The Woman in White's heels clicked as she walked in front of Ethan's anesthetized body, leaning forward, snapping her fingers in his face. Her lips curled at the sight of him being helpless. Slowly, her haunting walk beside Tatler fell menacing as she crossed her hands together.
"He's nearly out," she said.

Tatler grew enraged, thrusting himself towards Ethan, slapping him viciously. The pain rocked Ethan awake again. His body yielded to the sofa.

"No! Ethan! You have to be awake. We need you to remember..." Tatler pressed his head into the couch, and Ethan moaned at the intensity of the pain. "We need to bring the pieces out to make you whole." His head felt hotter now. He kept thinking, if he were to pass out, what would he do then?

The Woman in White caressed his cheek once more, gently blowing into his ear. Ethan couldn't help but be soothed by the relaxation. The drugs were running through his body, and it made his nerves tingle. "Relax," the Woman in White said calmly. And Ethan couldn't help but follow her command. His vision was drowned out as he felt himself being pulled into that awful memory.

The memory of her, and he couldn't resist. He fought, but the relaxation won, and Ethan had faded into his incubus.

Ethan begrudgingly opened the freezer. He didn't want to give her the satisfaction of grabbing the icepack and showing her how badly it hurt. She was so tuned to the television, hardly recognizing what she'd done, he knew she didn't care.

His arm jerked down as he winced from the pain. His rib felt on fire, and the swelling was setting in. Lifting his shirt to reveal a deep purple knot beginning to form.

He looked over to her, still entranced by the television. Sometimes he thought that if a passerby walked by the window, they'd think there was a normal mother and son on a Saturday afternoon. But the horror lay inside. The blackguard in his life reigned free. And his mind was his only escape.

Shuffling to his room, locking the door behind him. If not, she would surely break her trance-like state and question him on something stupid as an excuse to batter him. Ethan lay on his bed, his body jerking, applying the icepack carefully to his injury. Closed his eyes, drinking in the sunshine on his skin. The window in his view attracted him as the abandoned building behind his house caught his attention.

By that time, the building must have been vacant for three years. The outside was presumably as neglected as the inside. The unkempt weeds ran along in diverging directions. He thought he might need to escape just for some time, long enough for her to get in trouble; anything had to be better than where he was. And it was just for a night. She wouldn't notice. And he climbed through, hoping to momentarily escape the chaos as his memory blurred in.

Ethan centered back into reality as his memory was fully recalled now. Ethan felt uneasy as his stomach began to grow knots. He knew every thought and every pain he experienced was reality.

Ethan turned towards Tatler, slowly forming his words. "Where's the statue?"

Tatler chuckled, "What statue?"

Ethan pointed at the place that once held it. A perfect outline of dust indicated where the statue was placed. Tatler still remained calm. How could he? He must've known he'd be caught by now. Yet he grinned, questioning Ethan that he didn't possibly know what he was talking about.

Ethan stared at Tatler's wrist. His arms were covered by the long sleeves he wore. Ethan swallowed. Requesting this was sure to give him his answer, although he had to be sure.

"Show me your wrist." Ethan's face began to sweat as he slowly reached into his back pocket.

Tatler shook his head in annoyance. His demeanor changed as if he were another man.

"Why, Ethan?" Tatler looked down at his wrist, pulling his shirt up, revealing the scratches Ethan had given him days before. "You already knew the answer to that."

Ethan grabbed his phone, scrambling to unlock it before Tatler was able to grab it. Ethan was cornered. During the commotion, Tatler managed to block the door as Ethan was pressed in front of the bookshelf. He grabbed a heavy book, threateningly holding it over his head, ready to put it to use.

Tatler slowly walked towards the record player next to his chair, pressing play. A timely song played as Tatler closed his eyes and gently swayed his body to the music. Ethan eyed the door, wondering if he could make it. Even if he did, what if she was here? Waiting on the other side to knock him out now that he knew how deranged they were.

He had to try. I have to pick the right moment.

"What do you want?" Ethan shakily spoke, his body jittering to the menacing music.

Tatler slowly opened his eyes, still swaying. "To help you, of course." Tatler's face spread again. The smile that was once warming was now so maniacal.

"I DON'T WANT YOUR HELP!!!" Ethan's voice shrilled as the book started to weigh on him. His arm stiffened then sharply raised as the terror roused him.

"Why else would you come to me?" Tatler tapped the phone in his hand. "Once upon a time, there was a boy..."

Ethan's heart felt as if it was going to explode. Why is this 'Mad Man' telling him a story when he'll kill him after?

"...the boy visited his father at work. The father worked in a factory. A loud, loud factory, and the boy wandered off." Tatler slowly stopped swaying, continuing, "After a while, the boy was found; he had a gash in his back from a weapon. The weapon was an axe." Tatler's face was stiff as Ethan begged Tatler to let him go. Yet he proceeded..."They took the boy to the hospital, and when he awoke, he told them this—"

Tatler walked in front of the door, turning his body in Ethan's direction. Fuck. How was he supposed to have a shot at escaping now?

"He wandered off as children do and met a man. The man offered the boy candy if he followed him into a backroom. So the boy followed, although it wasn't sweets that awaited him. The boy was tricked. Once the boy realized the Man was lying, the Man pulled out an axe and slashed the boy's back." Tatler crossed his arms behind his back. This sick tale was ending, as was Ethan's chance.

"The Man heard screaming before he could kill the boy like he wanted. And even though the boy lived, he was stuck with a fear, a constant fear of that gruesome day, and that bloodied axe."

"You're deranged!" Ethan belted. The smile spread wider as if Tatler knew what he was doing was normal. To corner his patients and toy with their lives.

"One week," Tatler spoke with intention, like the manifesting videos Ethan would watch to give him confidence before a date.

"For what?" Ethan still held the book above his head, ready to throw it if Tatler decided to make a move.

But no, he stood still, and Ethan grew tired of his games. "Fuck you! Leave me alone!"

Tatler slowly placed one foot in front of the other, and each step felt like a death march. Ethan shouted for Tatler to stay back, but he ignored his commands. Ethan held the book up even higher, warning him of his fate if he was to move another inch in his direction.

Tatler reached into his pocket, pulling out Ethan's phone. Holding the device in front of him.

Ethan stared at it like prey, realizing the predator had him. "One week to beat the butterflies, Ethan." The warming smile was back.

Ethan slowly grabbed the phone out of his hand, afraid that if he was too slow, it was a trick. Cautiously, Ethan shifted his body weight towards the door.

Tatler remained still as he worked his way around him. Once he managed to sly around, Ethan bolted for the door, and Tatler still remained. Unfazed by the events that had just occurred.

Chapter Six
Paranoia

Ethan rapidly tapped his foot as he eyed the full glass of beer on the countertop. The bar was almost emptied, and when a patron entered, Ethan turned his entire body towards the bell ringing as some young drinkers or laborers came in from a long, hard day.

The sequence of tapping, looking, and checking for Tatler continued for twenty more minutes. The barman slapped his hand on the countertop, breaking Ethan's antsy trance. His body jerked from the sudden movement.

"Are you alright?" the barman asked.

Slowly looking up, Ethan knew the concern. He always finished his drink and appeared more on edge than usual.

Ethan gave a look reassuring the barman. Another ring of the doorbell. This time, a larger group than the last.

He rolled his eyes. The influx of new patrons was finally beginning to overwhelm him. Ethan stood up, the scraping sound of the stool heard as he turned and headed for the restroom.

Pushing the heavy door open, the air smelled of stale cleaning products. Ethan quickly dipped low to glance under every stall. *Great, no one here.*

He leaned his hands on the end of the sink and released a heavy sigh. The moments ran over and over in his mind.

All he could do was stare at the water dripping slowly from the faucet into the drain. Twice, Ethan tapped the sensor for the water to dispense, splashing it on his face, hoping to wake up from this nightmare world, to no avail.

What was he to do? Ethan looked up and froze. The reflection in the mirror made him freeze in fear from the sight of a pair of feet. The shoes were recognized instantly. Black oxfords. The shoes faced Ethan's direction and remained motionless.

Ethan slowly leaned up as he examined the slight view of a top hat at the top of the stall. Ethan turned around, blinking harshly, praying that what he was seeing was a fragment of his imagination.

He swallowed, the faint taste of beer was in his mouth, and he needed every ounce of courage. Ethan crept towards the stall. With every step he took, he prayed that the moment he opened the door, there would be nobody there. This whole week, he was going insane, and in an instant, he would wake up in a hospital, strapped down with people dressed in white and holding clipboards. But no, this was Ethan's reality, and it felt like a constant hell.

Ethan reached out, slowly grasping the lock. After a few moments, he felt the energy surge. Yanking the door open, Ethan's eyes expanded—a tall, stocky man stood in a panic after his moment of privacy was disturbed. His stocky build was no match for the average yet fit build of Tatler. And he had no hat. Ethan raised his hands in apology as the man stood exposed.

"I'm sorry," Ethan stumbled backwards, leaving the bar as the barman yelled for him to come back to pay his tab.

Chapter Seven
Monday

Ethan called out. No word from the police. Nothing. He had so many errands to run, pay off his monthly expenses: rent and car insurance.

Once the business was over, he planned to relax as he usually did, although that thought halted as the reality set in.

He remembered the words of Tatler, the feeling of being cornered, and the death march he made towards him. The events were running like a movie.

Ethan decided on a walk—yes, a walk would calm his nerves, he thought. Arriving at the park, the screams and shouting of children made him reminisce about his childhood.

Although not pleasant, jealousy always crept in as he saw the joy on their faces. All of them were perhaps experiencing a better childhood than he had.

He could hear the screams of his mother telling him to get up, as the thuds of him being kicked were drowning out. He was so in his head of memory he nearly bumped into Terry.

Terry smiled as he greeted Ethan. As a young woman approached, around Ethan's age, she still smelled of cheap perfume. She must be Cynthia, Ethan thought, as she carried a small white dog on her side, whose face constantly looked dirty as she stared at Terry. Ethan could tell they were most likely fighting moments before, and Terry was more obvious at covering up conflicts than she was.

"Hey, Terry." Ethan forced himself to remain calm as his palms began to build with sweat. Terry knew it instantly. Sometimes, Ethan swore he could be a psychic. Throwing Terry off was a rare feat, Ethan seldom achieved.

Ethan looked up at Cynthia, who shot back a disgusted look. He figured it was because he didn't truly acknowledge her.

"Hello, Cynthia."

She rolled her eyes as Ethan shyly waved. Terry nervously looked at Ethan.

"Scarlett," Terry corrected, rubbing his neck. His chest heaved up and down as she gave another sinister stare, he swore would cut through both of them.

Ethan looked apologetic as she set the puppy down. Hair was left on her dress as she untangled the leash before storming off.

Terry snickered reassuringly.

"Why aren't you at work?" Terry asked.

Ethan looked down, ashamed of his answer, so he decided to make one up, as most do.

"I felt sick," Ethan said. He felt it wasn't entirely a lie, considering the last few days. However, there was no comfort in telling the truth.

Ethan cleared his throat. "So why are you here today?"

Terry glanced at Scarlett, who was preoccupied with the pup. Ethan knew he wanted to answer once she was a safe distance away.

"Using a few vacation days," Terry muttered more under his breath. "To make up..."

Ethan acknowledged Terry's discomfort. The silence between the two was loud. Ethan hadn't noticed how much Terry was in thought. Perhaps just as much as Ethan.

Ethan scanned the park. Nothing seemed out of place at the moment. Kids were still playing, the sun was still up, and Terry was real.

He was sane.

Ethan closed his eyes, releasing another deep breath.

"What's going on, Ethan?" Terry leaned in, his arm coaxing Ethan's back as Ethan jerked away before scanning the park once more.

Terry ushered them to sit on a nearby bench.

The sun was causing the paint to peel over time. Ethan breathed deeply.

"Terry, you know I can be a little..." Ethan looked down, intertwining his fingers.

Terry sat composed, listening carefully to Ethan's words.

"...on edge." Another deep breath. "I thought I needed to work on it. Considering my childhood—anyway, I met this doctor and he's—deranged, to put it quite frankly. He's broken into my house, attacked me. And I can't prove it." Ethan closed his eyes as he soaked in the sun on his face. He didn't understand why confessing to Terry in this moment would help him now. Terry was in thought as he gave no reaction. He doesn't believe me.

Terry finally looked up. "Ethan, I think you're in jeopardy. Tell the police at least."

Ethan looked defeated. "How?" Ethan's face grew hot as the tears slid down his cheeks while Terry consoled him. Maybe it was the influx of his job or Tatler; either way, Ethan let it out.

Terry placed his hand on Ethan's back. A tenderness Ethan had been missing all his life. Just the presence of a friend.

Terry gently rubbed his back as Ethan was nearing the end of his relief. "If he is truly this deranged and no one will listen, then Ethan, you have to be brave." Ethan quickly wiped the tears from his face, wiping them against his worn jeans.

Whether he wanted to admit it or not, Tatler wasn't going to go away. He had a target, and that target was Ethan, whether he wanted him to be or not.

***

The TV played in the background, although Ethan paid no mind. He sat on his couch, completely focused on his laptop. A routine of looking at his screen and looking down to type something new. Over and over again.

He researched everything he could think of. The website, the office number, the address—and nothing. He had become a ghost. There's no way someone could just be erased like that. Ethan's mind started to flutter, and the crazy thoughts came. What if the police are in on it? What if Tatler and his goons are part of a cult?

His head sank. Another moment of defeat crept in like an intruder to an unsuspecting family in the night.

Dingggg!!! Dongggg!!!!

Ethan's body shot up. What now? He thought as he pushed the laptop aside. Walking towards the door and opening it.

A familiar man was already at his car as Ethan examined him further. The man reached for his car door in the same manner in a way he had reached for his money. Sebastian! Ethan sprinted, moving a hair short as Sebastian was already to his car and locked the door before Ethan had reached him.

He banged so hard the glass shook. "Sebastian?!"

He pulled away casually without another thought. The tires screeched, leaving marks on his driveway.

Ethan watched as the car sped away, the screeching still ringing in his ears. He turned towards his doorstep. A small brown box sat perfectly in the middle of his stoop. Ethan looked around it, hoping it wasn't wires of a mechanism to something to trigger and blow up.

Once he was sure, he lifted it firmly. A weight Ethan hadn't expected came. Using his force to push the door open and onto the living room counter.

He put his hands on his hips. What if something horrible, completely life-altering, was in this box? One minute went by, then two, ten, and Ethan still stared at it.

It was time. Enough bitching around. Pulling a knife from the kitchen drawer, he made the first incision. Cutting the tape, slowly opening the box.

Ethan was in horrific shock. His face froze; a large vintage camera lay on top of the images of himself, countless ones, of him going to work, getting groceries, some even days before he met Sebastian and Tatler, even the walk today of him and Terry.

The most shocking of all was of him bare-assed naked. He felt sick, and the detailed close-ups of his genitals pressed against the inflated dolls. Every scar Ethan had was photographed. Showcased like some animal at a circus.

Ethan seethed, his face was red, and the image of Tatler and the Woman in White was only on his mind.

"THOSE SICK FUCKS!!!" Ethan smashed the camera on his countertop. Hitting and kicking it on the ground until he saw only shards of pieces.

Pushing himself up, he boarded every window, door. All the entrances. He felt insane, yes, but his actions may keep him out.

Chapter Eight
Tuesday

Ethan shook his foot vigorously. The longer the Officer took to come back was another anxiety-filled thought that crept into his mind. He sat in the busy station, at a desk, across from the empty chair where the officer was supposed to be, but walked away to grab a cup of coffee.

"Want anything?" the Officer had said before Ethan had a moment to sit down. The clear worry on his face as he left without a second thought. Ethan was mad at first, although after a few minutes, he decided he may have needed a moment to collect his thoughts.

So he nibbled at his fingers and shook his leg vigorously, rummaging through the thoughts in his head. Finally, the heavy officer emerged carrying a croissant in his mouth, a coffee in one hand, and a stack of papers in the other. He slammed his body into his seat as the chair squealed, probably worn from the many times he sat his heavy weight into it. He sat back, intertwining his fingers over his belly that nearly hung over his belt. His badge appeared to pierce his chest.

"So what brings you in here, son?" he asked, licking his lips, poorly wiping the coffee off his mouth.

Ethan leaned up, letting spill what he'd been afraid of holding in. He confessed everything: the box, the mints, Doctor Tatler, and how everything started with that business card. Ethan dug in his pocket, pulling out the crumbled card and setting it on his desk. The Officer put on his thin-framed specs, closely examining them.

He shook the computer mouse, after a few seconds looked once more at the card and typed.

"There's no one by the name Elijah Tatler."

"What? How?" Ethan shook his head in denial. "What about the address?"

The Officer typed on. "It's an empty office building, son."

Ethan's eyes strained as they widened. There was no way it was an empty office space. "Go check it out, I'll show you." Ethan grew neurotic as the Officer remained uninterested.

Ethan appeared as if he hadn't slept for days. His eyes were puffy and baggy. His clothes seemed to have been thrown together, giving him a more tired look.

"There's no grounds for that." The Officer sighed in annoyance.

Ethan shook his head in denial once more. "Go search for it!"

The Officer remained still, and the commotion seemed not to shake him out of his slackened state, as if Ethan was having a tantrum and not being harassed and targeted by a deluded psychopath.

"Mr. Bedford, unless you can bring me probable cause, there's nothing I can do." Ethan thought of the images of his naked body; out of all the pictures, those would raise his eyebrow, but Ethan couldn't bring himself to do it. The feeling of someone examining him so vulnerable was too much for him to bear.

He was so in thought, he hadn't heard the Officer ask, "Do you have any evidence?" Ethan stared, the clamming of his body returned, and he knew he didn't want to have an attack there. He shook his foot and repeated the mantras in his mind that would work for some time: Deep breaths. 1...2...3...

His mind flashed with uncertainty. He could see through the shattered window in the distance, the police questioning his mother. They were too far for him to read their lips, but he knew the reason they were there. It was only a matter of time before they knew his hideaway.Ethan hadn't been to school in a week, and she had been too dissociated to realize it. The building was dank and cold, yet it was warmer than he had ever been living with her. He looked around at his blanket and a few items he had gradually taken from his bedroom, trying to make it feel like home anyway he could.

Ethan shifted in his seat as his stare grew blank. The officer waved his hands, trying to catch Ethan's attention. "Son? Do you have any evidence?" the officer spoke.

"I can't help you." The chair squealed under the Officer as he leaned forward, typing away on his computer. Ethan slammed his fist on the desk. Being ignored was not what he had in mind. The Officer's mustache furrowed as Ethan got up, pushing his chair back so badly it almost tipped over. Balling his fist, letting him know of his dissatisfaction before leaving.

Ethan forcefully pushed the door open. Outside was even louder but more calming. The feeling of being judged for seeking help made Ethan feel angered again.

Maybe he felt that way because of her. The memory crept in. He'd remember the moments when Police would arrive at his house and his mother would answer the door, frantic. Her hair was never done, and he was always smelly from days without a shower. The uniforms made him think he'd be safe this time. No yelling, no hiding from the pain she caused, but it never happened—he was always stuck with her, and he hated them for it.

Ethan lit a cigarette, softly inhaling the bitter taste of his bud. The comfort of relief was back; he didn't have to think of—

The car was approaching, the same black Cadillac as Tatler's. Slowly, Ethan dropped the cigarette on the ground and crushed it, twisting his shoe into the pavement. He turned and walked. Maybe it was just a random car until the car slowed its pace. Ethan turned around as the car stopped. He debated whether he should go back into the station. Staring back and forth at the door and the black Cadillac. Tatler could cut him off if he wanted, considering how far he had walked away from any help.

Ethan walked a few more paces, and the car rolled slowly once more. Ethan stopped, hearing the sounds of the tires halting on the gravel. Ethan removed his hands from his pockets. Backing up a few more feet, he ran. The car started up, and the screeching of the tires raced as Ethan rounded a corner. The parking lot where his car was finally came into view.

If only Ethan had his keys out like he usually did, he could click the panic button and alert someone. Frantically searching his body as the car whipped in front of him, nearly hitting him, blocking his access to his vehicle. The door swung open, and Tatler emerged. His menacing smile spread across his face.

Ethan began to yell as Tatler punched him in the jaw. His mouth began to fill with the taste of metal. The stinging followed as Tatler pinned Ethan against the doctor's car, taking hold of his face.

Ethan was dazed as he spoke, "Why are you fucking doing this?"

Tatler squeezed his face harder, making sure Ethan could look him in the eyes. "You're going to thank me for this someday." Tatler deeply sniffed Ethan, the natural fumes giving Tatler a rapturous feeling.

Ethan pushed him off, throwing his fist towards him but wildly missing. Tatler caught it, squeezing so tightly that Ethan thought his arm might break.

"Please..." Ethan begged; the pain was excruciating.

Tatler let go, gently lingering over him as Ethan fell to the floor, grasping his arm. Tatler sneered as if he had procured a tremendous victory over Ethan. Tatler stepped over him, opening the car door, sat inside, still smiling crudely at him, and sped off.

Chapter Nine
Wednesday

Ethan stared at Tatler's office. The building was still new, but now empty. The letters printed on Tatler's name were gone.

He saw nothing but black windows and knew there was no one. Like it never happened. Tatler didn't bait him into thinking he would be cured from his constant wallowing in life.

Ethan leaned back into his seat, blasting the air conditioning. The moment was approaching for him to be brave. No challenge was greater. And yet he still remained in his vehicle, parked far, and reran his thoughts about what to do.

Okay, go in and find evidence.

And the next sensible thought came. What am I looking for?

If anything was even there. What if he broke in and set off an alarm? Or Tatler and that crazy bitch was there, waiting.

Either way, it was time; he stalled long enough. Every bone in his body wanted to retreat, yet he opened his door, stepping one foot on the pavement.

His head looked around quickly as he peeked out. It was an empty parking lot, yes, although Tatler always seemed to get the jump on him. Fully standing, Ethan scanned once more. A bird flew over, startling him, its talons nearly scraping the top of his head. Ethan watched it land perfectly in the middle of the office building.

Watching him as if he were a gladiator in for the last fight of his life, Tatler's office being the arena.

Ethan slowly paced his way to the door. A tingle ran through his body as he placed his hand on the handle, gently pulling to not triggering the sound of the wind rushing into the place.

The place was quiet, quieter than usual. The immediate reaction was his realizing the furniture was empty. The office felt hollow, with a sense of dread.

Ethan walked to where the receptionist's desk was, peering over to nothing. The outlets lay bare as he checked any corner that may hide a laptop.

Nothing. And Ethan knew the next and perhaps only place to check: Tatler's office. That same office he was cornered in days before, the same office he was drugged in, and the place where he met the insane Mad Man.

The red light that hung above the office turned on again. He thought possibly someone was here to trigger it until Ethan's sleeve caught onto a small switch tucked away behind the desk. Ethan flicked the switch, and the red light turned off. He flicked it once more, the light turning on simultaneously.

Ethan stared at the office, praying it'd be over quickly. Softly, he pushed the door, making sure not to creak it. The office was the same. The dread filled Ethan again. This place should've been a haven for those who seek it. But no, Tatler robbed him of that as a man would rob a woman of dignity.

His goal was the computer, yet Ethan's eyes went towards the candy bowl. Those awfully tasting green-wrapped mints that Ethan knew were anything but.

Ethan rushed towards the table, snatching handfuls of the candies and shoving them into his pockets. Some spilled onto the table and some onto the floor. All he needed was to talk to a doctor. A real doctor and tell them he was drugged. They'd believe him. Those mints had to have been laced.

Right now, Ethan had to remain focused; the computer sat open on his desk. Ethan sat in the chair and wiggled the mouse to awaken the screen. A roadblock lay ahead. PASSWORD REQUIRED.

You got to be fucking kidding me! Ethan banged his hand on the desk. Of course, a password was needed. A man like Tatler wouldn't leave his desktop unlocked.

Ethan's mind raced. What was that damn password? Ethan first tried: (Tatler, Elijah Tatler, Deranged psychopath.)

Error. Please try again.

Ethan thought hard; he thought maybe this could be stupid, still, he typed it. Ethan Bedford.

It unlocked.

A small sense of relief washed over Ethan, grateful he was that obsessive.

The home screen was blue, and two files were displayed, one named "Ethan" and the other named "Gregory."

Ethan clicked on his own: empty. Ethan felt heavy. What was he planning for? An empty file and two days left for whatever Tatler had planned for Ethan. No, Ethan knew whatever it was, he wasn't going to fall for it; he just needed evidence and to expose Tatler for what he was.

Exiting out, he clicked on the only other file there, labeled "Gregory." Ethan was appalled; the images that lay before him were of a man slightly younger than Ethan. Photos of him being stalked, similar to what Ethan experienced. Casually, then slowly, Gregory's demeanor changed. A constant paranoia stained his face. As he scrolled, horror glazed his face. News headline from twenty years ago. It read: Local Boy, Eight Years of Age, Deceived by Production Worker, Nearly Killed.

The article went on: A young boy, Gregory Matthias, was attacked earlier today by his father's co-worker at his father's place of work. The boy was invited by his father to shadow him at his work, but the boy wandered off. Seemingly, the boy was met by local production worker Kurt Pataki, who lured the boy into a room, attacking him with an axe. The boy was injured and quickly taken to a local hospital. The family has declined to comment. We have tried to make contact with Mr. Pataki, who also declined to comment on his reasons for attacking the boy. Sources say the boy is in a comatose state—

The words rang in Ethan's head: "The boy" and "axe." Those keywords stayed with Ethan.

This was the story Ethan didn't want to listen to that Tatler forced him to hear. That fucker. Ethan's mind raced again. Whatever he did to Gregory was what he was sure to do to Ethan. And he had to find out what.

He scrolled again; there were notes on pages someone had written. He recognized the handwriting. Tatler had written pages and pages of information about Gregory, every detail, it seemed, of his life, things you'd never tell anyone.

Names, so many names of people he encountered and how much of an impact they might have had. The constant images of a man who would sell him coffee every morning. Where he'd most likely be every day and what time. The things he was most afraid of:

The axe was broad-beveled, 3 inches, and rustic, slightly; the handle had a chip at the bottom, possibly passed down to Pataki.

Ethan felt sick; it was as if Tatler knew everything about Gregory. He was studying his prey as if he wanted to embody him, to know every step and think of every outlet possible.

He scrolled more, glazing over the notes Tatler made after each session. The end was ghastly; Ethan froze in shock. It was of Gregory looking back in a panic; he knew the feeling instantly. Tatler was following him.

The following image was of Gregory pushing his way into an abandoned factory, similar to the one where he was attacked as a child, although this one was nearly destroyed, erosion over time and weather had got to it.

The next image: Gregory was hiding poorly behind an old machine; he could tell Tatler was playing with him, watching him and giving a slice of hope, making him feel he had no known where he was.

Ethan didn't want to look, but he had to. What if this is exactly what Tatler was planning, a foreshadowing of Ethan's fate? So he scrolled; the image of Gregory limping, his body covered in sweat from the panic and chase, and his calf bleeding out. He knew the end was nearly for him.

Another photo was of Tatler remaining still as Gregory had given distance, but Ethan knew Tatler remained behind to toy with him. He knew at any moment Tatler could lift his axe and end it then and there. But no, that sick game he wanted to play, no one else did. This was fun for him. An additional image was Gregory in the far distance; he was lying on the ground, seemingly passed out from the pain. His body looked already lifeless, and Tatler wanted to capitalize on it.

The last image of Gregory, bloodied, the axe laid next to him. Tatler hovered about him, admiring the work he had done. Ethan couldn't believe what he saw; this deranged psycho knew everything about him. His face grew horrified as the air grew thick around him. Every breath choked on air as he tried to calm himself down.

Why me? The thought-provoking question seemed to be on all week.

Out of everyone in the world, it had to be him.

Ethan pulled out his phone and captured every image or note he could find. There was no way he was going to allow himself to be next. Refused to let the next person think, Poor Bastard, as he thought for Gregory.

Ethan froze as the sound of the lobby door opening reached his ears. Ethan quietly scooted off the chair, keeping low to the ground to remain undetected. Slowly crawling to the door, steadily closing it nearly shut, peering through a crack.

The Woman in White walked down the opposite hall. Her morbid walk gave a menacing appeal. She passed two doors and entered a room. Ethan knew it was his chance to see. He got up and cautiously crept down the hall, pressing himself against the walls. He knew it would be useless if she came out at any moment; the hall was too exposed, and Ethan wasn't thin enough to press his body against the pillars.

Ethan approached the door, and through the glass, he could see the Woman in White. She sat rummaging through a desk. Finally pulling out a silver laptop. Placing it on top of the desk. A video was already displayed; gently caressing her finger over the pad, she pressed play.

A wave of disgust befell him. It was Ethan standing in the kitchen of his home, the day he made himself a cup of hot chocolate because Christmas was nearing, and he tried to force himself to get into the holiday spirit. Even though Ethan hated hot chocolate, he made the cup so hot that the liquid burned his tongue, causing him to jerk his cup, spilling the scalding liquid onto his shirt. He still remembered that day, a stupid day of spilling his mug because his coffee was too hot. To go back, to not accept that stupid card from Sebastian. But no, he had to watch this sick woman.

She stopped the video, and Ethan held his breath, praying not to make a peep.

She scanned for more videos, the abundance of recordings she had of him over the last year. She clicked another; Ethan was home, being placed in his bed by Tatler and Sebastian. He was asleep under the drug-induced haze Tatler had tricked him into from the mints.

The Woman in White shook the camera as she set it on Ethan's dresser. The three of them stood around him in formidable stances as he lay helpless. Tatler gently caressed his cheek before kissing him on the forehead and leaving. Sebastian followed shortly behind.

The sickest thing of all, Ethan watched the Woman in White through the window as she pushed her sleeve down.

The video began to show her now, quietly looking back before sitting on his bed. Biting her lip as she began to remove Ethan's clothes. His exposed body did not react as the drugs were surely in effect.

He grew sick, almost wanting to vomit at the sight of him being touched. She lay on top of him, running her fingers gently across his skin.

Tears welled in Ethan's eyes; the insanity of that woman to violate him like that. He couldn't react, just watching as the Woman in White pulled her dress down to her hips, exposing her breasts. She reached out, grabbing a tube of lipstick, pulling the top off.

Twisting it up to show the last of her crimson color. Gently and finely pressing it to her lips. Tracing the last of the color out. Like she had to watch herself to feel power.

She watched herself slyly teasing Ethan, kissing and licking his scars with slight nibbles, her fingers dancing on his skin.

Ethan began to fester with rage. Balling his fist. The angst of her, her sick mind thinking she could do that to him. Ethan's mind spiraled from envisioning the vile things he wanted to inflict on her.

But he couldn't, at least not yet. Ethan unclenched his fist, forcing himself to remain calm. He peeked over.

Her hands reached down, watching her body submit to her fingers, giving her pleasure as the visual of a helpless Ethan was being violated.

The screen turned black, and for a split second, the reflection of Ethan was shown through the glass.

The Woman in White turned her head to no one when looking towards the door.

Quickly, she dressed herself and exited the room to the empty hallway. A moment went by, and she remained still before realizing the red light was on above Tatler's office.

Ethan stood still and carefully managed to hide in a room he was grateful was unlocked before the Woman in White swung open her door, making him feel cornered once more.

The sounds of her heels rang as she flew open Tatler's door. The sight of mints scattered about made her smirk. She slowly sauntered out of the room, closing the door behind her.

"I know you're still here," her voice had a menacing smoothness to it. Same as a predator trying to coax its prey into giving up.

Ambling down the hall. Peeking into the first room. No one was there; she closed the door and slowly started again. Her voice, speaking with harboring feels, "Do I remind you of your mother?" She playfully tugged her sleeve down again.

Ethan's temper spiked again. Never once did his mother touch him in that way. All Ethan could remember were the beatings, the pushing that turned to kicks and fists as he grew older. The reason for his scars—no, he couldn't think of that right now. The only thing he needed was an escape. A way to get past her.

Breathe, Ethan, breathe.

All he had to do was utilize what he had and think. Ethan's eyes zoomed around the room. A large brown box sat in the corner; quietly kneeling, he rummaged through it. Feeling for a weapon, a can of aerosol, anything. The room was so dark he couldn't risk turning on the light, knowing she was two doors away. He needed this time to feel for—Got it!

Ethan pulled out a statue similar to the one she used to put him in his daze. This statue was slightly heavier, and now Ethan had to get ready. She was one room away from Ethan now, and all he could feel was his heart racing.

"You saw me? How do I make you feel good?" her voice lowered as she entered the room just before Ethan. "I know it wasn't part of the plan, yet I feel so feral, Ethan."

Ethan took a deep breath; her footsteps were within a few feet of him now. He had one chance, and he couldn't fuck it up.

The woman stood at the door. Opening the door, Ethan stood behind. The tension nearly eating at him as he watched her step inside, Ethan thrust his arm down, clubbing her in the back of her head.

She collapsed, and Ethan kneeled on top, shaking her violently. "Why are you doing this?!"

Ethan shook her again. Her head began to be covered in red, nearly matching her lipstick.

Ethan felt the warmth of it. It slowly started to flood more, and Ethan still shook her, and her head rocked back and forth. "Why?!" Her mouth spread a menacing smile, the same one she shared with Tatler.

She gently reached for Ethan's face, caressing his cheek; her arm fell, and her eyes slowly closed.

Ethan's hands lifted, coated in red. The angst won, and he felt it slowly dissipate. He remained in disbelief as he realized what he had done.

The door swung open once more; the familiar sound of suede shoes was back, and he knew instantly who it was. Tatler.

Ethan stammered back, quickly rounding the corner nearest to him. Ethan stared at the sunlight reflecting on his shirt. Tracing the light coming from a small room across from him. Through the small crack of a window. His heart fluttered. A way out.

The footsteps grew faint; he knew Tatler was in his office, and now was Ethan's chance. He knew he'd only have three, maybe five seconds before Tatler saw the candies scattered about.

Ethan rushed for the window, pushing on it as it fought back. Ethan gritted his teeth, pressing harder and harder until finally it opened, and Ethan yielded all his might to crawl through.

Within an instant, Tatler knew something was off the moment the candies were spattered about. His office always remained clean because she hated a mess. The first slam of the window caught Tatler's attention. He rushed out to the hall, seeing her lying there. Rushing to her side, she was gone, a slight smirk bestowed on her as if she found her last pleasure. Gently lifting her up into his arms.

Positioning her head to face him, Tatler held her. The screeching sound of a car peeling off made him jerk up. Tatler closed his eyes, knowing exactly who was to blame.

Ethan paced fast into his workplace, looking more frantic than usual. He didn't care, didn't care what co-workers called him crazy.

He viciously pressed the elevator button; a few others were waiting for it although decided to hang back once they saw Ethan's state. Once the door opened, he quickly retreated his hands under his shirt, hoping no one saw the bits of blood stain that he had poorly washed off in the parking lot moments before.

The elevator closed; Ethan threw his arms to his sides. A moment to breathe again. It was only a matter of time before Tatler was on to him. The doors opened, and Ethan paced towards his desk. The awful stench hit him. So foul he thought he would vomit. His coworkers walked frantic with their mouths covered as he sat.

The rotten stench of eggs, like someone had died, he thought. Ethan pulled out his drawer, knowing that finding anything that would deafen the smell. Ethan pulled on the three-tier drawer, the first two having nothing but paperwork.

Ethan covered his mouth harder, the smell growing more as he leaned down. He opened the drawer; the puppy he fed every morning lay bloodied, his head bashed.

Ethan slammed the cabinet closed, looking around hectically to make sure no one saw the devastation laid on his desk. Tears ran down his cheeks as he puffed for air. No—no. Frantically pulled out his phone and opened the photos app. Tapping on the most recent one and reviewing.

In his search, he tried his best to research what could be about Gregory, his work, his family, anything. Nothing—all his attempts were dead ends. Did Tatler erase their brains too? No, no one could be that elaborate, yet Ethan felt anything was possible at this point.

Ethan felt he was missing something, so he swiped through the images. The coffee shop the man where Gregory met every day.

Ethan intensely zoomed in on the slight blur of the patch on the barista's shirt. Barely making out the name, he was slowly typing in letter by letter. Hoping that when the screen loaded, his curiosity would finally be rewarded. One shop was listed, and Ethan lifted the phone on his desk. Pressing the number into the dial pad.

Ringing twice before a soft female voice answered. Ethan frantically spoke, feeling the woman's bewilderment.

"Hi, uh, is there a man by the name—" Ethan zoomed more into the image, squinting at his nametag.

"—Adam?" A pause filled the room as she hesitantly responded.

His face started to redden as Ethan forced the words out. "You're going... to jail."

Tatler tightened his grip. "Oh really?" He searched Ethan's body, pulling out the phone. Tatler's expression gleamed as he waved the phone in Ethan's face, having it unlock.

"Nooo!"

"What did you expect?" Tatler deleted the photos. Ethan's sense of panic rushed over him.

Tatler smiled, pulling Ethan forward and banging his head into the wall, rocking the elevator.

A surge of fear surged through Ethan as he watched the elevator doors open. Two peers raced out, desperately covering their mouths. The retched smell made them gag.

"Uhhh..." Ethan pondered, knowing he had no time to delegate as the line remained quiet.

"A friend." Immediately regretted the answer. "It's an emergency!" Ethan added.

A short delay of silence was on the other end until she called out. "Adam! A crazy guy is on the phone asking for you!" Ethan had no time for offense as he heard the phone exchange hands. His voice was croaky as he answered. Possibly fitting the image of the man in the photo, right?

"Hello? This is Adam." Ethan smiled in relief, like a player scoring a goal.

"Hello? I'm Ethan. I know this will sound crazy, but—" He breathed deeply. "Do you remember the customer by the name Gregory?" he asked in earnest.

"Yeah, he used to come by all the time." Ethan frowned. Used to.

"I have to get back to customers now."

Ethan pleaded, "No! No! Please!" his hands rose as if Adam was standing in front of him. If he begged hard enough, he could feel the torture in his cry for help.

Adam sighed, asking what else he needed.

"Do you remember anything about him?" Ethan watched the elevator once more as another coworker ran inside, escaping the horrid smell of the pooch in his cabinet.

"No, he just bought coffee. That's it."

Ethan scowled at the answer. The disappointment was setting in, and defeat was closing behind.

"Please, tell me anything. I could really use the help."

Adam contemplated hard. "He did mention he used to work for a Pest control company shortly before he stopped coming here. Pest Co."

Yes! Ethan cheered internally. Thanking Adam over and over before hanging up. A small victory, but a victory nonetheless. Ethan typed once more the address, pressing print, holding out his hand as the paper slowly released from the machine.

A familiar floral scent engulfed his nose. Her large form covered Ethan's sight of the elevator door he occasionally eyed. "Look who's here yet called out for the last three days," She held a stack of papers on her side that seemed to disappear halfway through, swallowed by her arm. Her face scrunched. "It seems the smell is worse at your desk."

Ethan eyed his cabinet as he folded the paper, shoving it into his front pocket. Lifting himself from the chair, only to be blocked by Janice.

"You expect me to believe you're sick? You look perfectly fine."

Ethan rolled his eyes, which Janice caught, which only made her fragile ego surge.

"Excuse me?" Waving a finger in his face. The faint smell of frosting flowed past Ethan.

His face furrowed, and Ethan clenched his fist. Festering as his face turned red. Janice wasn't about to have power any longer.

"SHUT UP, YOU FAT BITCH!" Ethan puffed, his hands released. The angst towards Janice was long overdue.

The co-workers stared on in shock, some smiling; Ethan bestowed what most wanted to do for ages.

Ethan spoke once more, this time staring straight into Janice's eyes. "Move!" He said firmly.

Janice slowly stepped aside; he didn't care if he was fired or if she were to report him, and the cops were to be there in five minutes. This moment was enough to fuel him for ages.

Ethan confidently walked to the elevator door, not staring at anyone but knowing he was the center of attention.

The doors opened, and he leaned his head against the wall.

A new feeling washed over Ethan, a release he hadn't felt in forever. It didn't compare to the warmth of a woman or the feel of a medicated high from a drug.

Ethan breathed and breathed as the floor hit the second level.

The doors opened, and Ethan waited for the next patron to step on the elevator, hoping it was Terry. A smile on his face he couldn't break.

The door opened; immediately, he stepped in. Grabbing Ethan's throat and slamming him against the wall.

He squeezed as Ethan struggled, pressing his body more if Ethan dared to move.

"Little piggy." Tatler's eyes flickered. A rage awakened in him. "You think you're winning, huh?"

Ethan pushed Tatler back. His body reacts slowly to capitalize as Tatler rams Ethan's body back into the steel bar on the wall. Wrapping his hands around his neck once again.

Ethan grabbed him, his force not shaking Tatler from breaking his grasp. He squeezed. His face started to redden as Ethan forced the words out. "You're going... to jail."

Tatler smiled, pulling Ethan forward and banging his head into the wall, rocking the elevator.

Ethan could see the emergency button as Tatler leaned in close, still squeezing Ethan's neck.

"For?" Tatler squeezed harder, his hands clung on as Ethan's feet lifted. Inches away from the button.

"Gregory...I know—you killed him." Ethan heard a ringing. If he didn't reach the button, he was sure to fade.

Tatler released one hand from Ethan, reaching into his front pocket. Frantically digging for the paper. "You still don't understand." Ethan regained a bit as Tatler shoved the paper into his mouth and swallowed.

Ethan pushed Tatler back once more, kicking the button so hard it broke.

A deafening screech poured as the elevator came to a screeching halt. Both cascaded down as the light dawned over them. Sprawled from the harsh impact.

Ethan slowly awoke, instantly grabbing at the surging pain on the back of his head.

The elevator was dark, and the overhead flickered rapidly. Ethan realized Tatler was still unconscious; quickly, it was his time to act. He sharply reached for his phone. Ethan strained as he pushed himself up, breathing in between the movements before reaching the door. Readying himself before correcting his stance, he dug his fingers into the doors and pulled.

Occasionally, looking back to make sure Tatler hadn't awoken. Ethan gritted his teeth as he pulled and pulled. The whites of his fingers showed; the blood rushed back when he stopped, and the pain felt like needles in his nails.

He refused to give up. He pulled and he pulled until—light! A thin strip of light on the floor showed, giving Ethan the fuel he needed.

Tatler coughed; Ethan looked back and grunted, pulling the doors apart far enough for his body to shimmy through.

Come on! Come on!

His body felt compressed as he fought through the pain. Tatler shook his head. His body is still trying to keep up.

Ethan pressed the last of himself through; the next step might have been the hardest. Ethan pressed his hands against the cold doors and pushed inward, slowly closing Tatler's window for escape.

Tatler wiped the blood from his eye. Now with vision, he saw Ethan closing his window.

"No!"

Tatler pressed his body up, fighting through his haze. Ethan had a few inches left before the doors closed, and Tatler was now getting his bearings. Yet Ethan pushed and pushed; slowly, the door closed as Tatler was left stranded.

Ethan ran up the stairs.

The muffled sounds of Tatler screaming, kicking and punching from the other side as Tatler pulled on the doors.

Ethan scrambled for the keys, pulling them out of his pocket, pulling for the door, hopping in and driving away.

Wildly peeling onto the road, praying he was going the speed limit, although he doubted it. His head and nerves were on fire. A green light switched to red, having Ethan slam on the brakes; he knew he wanted to keep going, although what a way.

Ethan felt eyes on him again, looking over to a disheveled Tatler in the black Cadillac. He waved a phone in his hand. Dialing a few moments later, an unknown number emerged.

Ethan answered, pressing the phone against his face.

"I'm growing bored, Ethan." Ethan looked over as he shouted, "Fuck you!" causing Tatler to snicker. "See, can't even be original. Good luck, Ethan." The phone call died. Ethan watched Tatler as he reversed his car, positioning it a hundred feet behind Ethan. He slammed the gas as the rubber on the tires burned. Ethan knew he was trying to ram him, that sick bastard. Ethan slammed on the gas, creating dust between him and Tatler.

Ethan maneuvered, cut corners, anything to throw Tatler off, and yet Tatler remained several spaces behind.

Ethan's eyes veered as a traffic jam was ahead; what was he to do if Tatler caught him?

Ethan screeched to a halt, nearly hitting the dark blue SUV that had one too many political stickers on it. The left side had a dent that someone wrote ("Oppsies") in faded Sharpie.

Ethan honked frantically, yelling at the pace of cars taking their time. The driver stepped out, a tall man with a handlebar mustache and dirty construction clothes.

Waving his hands in an intimidating manner. Ethan honked, screaming for him to move. The man hit his window repeatedly; Ethan tuned it out. The rearview window grabbed all his attention as the black Cadillac was approaching.

He put his gear shift in reverse; the driver was still angrily slapping the window. Ethan eagerly signaled for him to go back in his car, the chain reaction of cars honking as he panicked. The driver stepped back, lifting his leg, spiking his boot at Ethan's car.

Ethan yelled, "Go back to your car!" But the driver heard nothing but his boot connecting with the door. The driver pulled his leg back once more, preparing his anger at Ethan's window.

The Cadillac slammed into the man, a loud thump as Ethan stared on in sheer horror. Tatler looked over, backing up as if the man were a simple speed bump. Ethan reversed as onlookers exited their cars. Plowing his car forward as Tatler menacingly stared off, while the car grew distant.

Chapter Ten
Thursday

Ethan tapped the peeling steering wheel, locking eyes on the building before him. If he thought nice things, he'd almost forget the patient was inside it.

His brow was sweaty, and every time he wiped, it reappeared. Out of this entire week, this was the most scared he'd been. He contemplated his reasons for being here, and maybe it was experiencing near-death, but his conscience couldn't shake it.

His bones vibrated as he slowly pushed the door open, stepping onto the cobblestoned pathway that led to the entrance.

The air pushed him back, maybe a sign to get in the car and drive away. His last warning before he faced her.

Entering the lobby was cold, and various workers in scrubs quickly paced in and out of the room, all having a goal in mind.

Ethan turned his attention towards the reception desk. The young lady typed as he approached, looking up as a welcome. Her face was pleasant and cheerful compared to the tension appearing on Ethan's.

"How may I help you?" her smile gleaming.

Ethan pressed his fingers into the countertops, hoping the words would spill out. Every other moment, he swallowed.

"Here to see Heidi Bedford." His heart sped up.

She typed and scrolled, nodding.

"And you are?"

"Her son." Ethan showed his ID to her, flashing the plastic card.

She typed again. "Room 402."

Ethan shook his head, proceeding to walk through the wave of workers. A variety of patients are laughing at visitors and orderlies helping the weaker ones into the beds.

Ethan tried to stare straight; every step he took felt weaker. The smell of cleaning products filled his lungs.

The room door was cracked slightly open and made a slight squeak as Ethan pushed it open.

The thin woman looked out the window, not noticing the squeak of the door or the chatter of people walking past.

Ethan leaned against the threshold, knocking softly.

Heidi turned around, to an instant wave of regret and excitement washed over her face.

She looked pale and tired. The wrinkles creased more as she gave Ethan a half-hearted smile. It only made him retreat into himself as if the little boy in him had to face the monster in his closet. The pit feeling in his belly was back, and he could feel the trigger coming.

The monster now was her, the woman he called Mom. All he wanted to do was run, but it was time.

"Ethan?" Heidi softly spoke, reaching her hand out as Ethan still stood in the doorway. Hesitation ate at him. He looked down as the words stuttered out, "...mom."

Her eyes lit up, the word she hadn't heard in what felt like forever. Her smile fell again once the pain on his face showed.

Heidi pointed at the empty seat across the room.

"Did you want to sit?" she said pleadingly.

Ethan shook his head, refusing. The silence grew for a while as Ethan was in his thoughts, knowing she was trying to smooth over or perhaps rewrite history.

"You look so different now." She smiled. "What's it been? Ten years?"

Ethan clasped his hands. "Twelve."

Heidi lowered her head, and the tears fell. The sniffing was causing her body to jerk rhythmically.

Ethan pondered; his hands felt raw as he clenched them. "Stop! Just stop!" He bellowed, refusing to have her feel sorry. She wiped the tears from her face as his eyes seized.

"You have no right." Ethan walked closer to her; his demeanor changed, and his pain was released. A pain deep inside him grew as the tears fell from his face onto the floor. His mouth tasted salty, and his throat hurt as he forced himself to express the words.

"The things you did—" Ethan's words lost as Heidi pleaded. Her hands clasped over her chest. "I know I haven't been a good mom to you, but I was mentally unfit to be your mother." Ethan's heart sank; slowly, it filled with a fire he held for so long it almost felt like forever. "Bullshit! You always refused help. And when I would point anything out to you, it was a punishment."

Heidi sobbed as he continued on, shaking her head in denial at the horrid things he spewed.

"...I know you remember stuffing my head underwater, the beatings when I begged you to stop—" Ethan rubbed his stomach to the wounds that never healed. "Burning me when I wailed in pain to my skin searing." The tears flowed out. "...The smell of my flesh is still burned into my nostrils. What child deserved that?!"

The silence filled the room again. Heidi was fetaled as she tried to erase the grotesque things she did. Her tears fell faster than she could wipe away. Heidi bit her lip, trying to think of what to say. It was too fragile for her to break the tension, yet she knew the state was make or break.

"I'm proud of you. Whether I've shown you or not. I do love you, Ethan." Ethan tapped his leg, nodding his head. How could he give closure to someone who hurt him so bad?

"Truly, I don't know if I can forgive you." Ethan wiped the final tear. "Honestly, I don't know why I'm here." Ethan walked out and sprinted down the hall.

Heidi stood up, pleading once more, "Ethan, please! I'm Sorry!" His figure faded from her view as she sat on the edge of her bed, leaning forward, dropping her head down in her hands.

Harsh footsteps entered her room, followed by the door closing. Heidi lifted her head, confused.

Tatler stood at the end of the room. "I'm glad he stood up to you." Tatler dug into his pocket, pulling out a bloodstained handkerchief, wiping it across the open cut on his forehead. "His progress is growing just as I had hoped." Tatler looked through the small window on the door, making sure they wouldn't be disturbed.

Slowly, Tatler walked towards Heidi. "Who are you?" Tatler sat on the bed, giving Heidi a menacing smile. "I'm here to help." Tatler grabbed the pillow, pushing it onto Heidi. Her kicks and screams grew muffled as Tatler pressed his weight onto her. His loins became hard as he pressed her body into the bed more.

She slowly, with time, stopped flailing. Tatler removed the pillow from the scarred eyes she had stained on her face, her face covered in saliva from the screams she tried to escape from her body.

Tatler got up, placing her neatly back into bed, gently caressing her hair. Tatler unzipped his pants, wrapping his hand around himself and fed into his arousal. Tugging up and down as he gasped in relief.

His breathing slowed as he came off his euphoric high. Pulling his pants on and zipping himself as if it never happened.

Chapter Eleven
Friday

Ethan turned onto his street. The flashes of red and blue lights filled the air, and police cars nearly blocked the road.

The further he got down the road, the more worry he felt as they piled into his driveway.

Two officers talked at his front door as he parked, waiting for him to approach.

"What's going on?" Ethan peered over the officers, realizing his door was mangled, barely holding up on one hinge.

"Mr. Bedford, witnesses say a man was seen forcing entry into your home about an hour ago," the other officer said. "They said he was wearing a top hat and described him as a white male. Does it ring any bells?"

Ethan breathed deeply, cautiously entering his home, stepping on the shards of wood from the door.

The scene was worse than any bar day or any drunken stupor Ethan had ever been in. The entire house was dismantled as if a wrecking ball had been pushed around ten times.

The gashes in the wall created by an axe, anything made of glass or electronic was smashed into pieces.

One of the officers walked towards the hallway, guiding Ethan to his bedroom.

Ethan's stomach knotted. Two human-sized dolls lay on his bed, one slightly shorter than the other, dark hair like Ethan's, covered in blood and slash marks. The other was sporting a poorly matted blonde wig and a rope around her neck.

"Any idea as to who would do this, Mr. Bedford?" The officer stared him down as if he were to burn a hole in him. Yet his demeanor remained more still than a statue.

The scene of what was supposed to be him and his mother. The oddity of it all. He thought maybe it was because hours before, the Woman in White was alive, and now the constant replay of her smile as her life drained out.

"Mr. Bedford?" Ethan looked up, breaking the trance he was locked into. Ethan looked motionless at the officer. "No, I don't know who could do this."

The second officer grasped at his belt, the hefty items causing them to clank together.

"Are you sure? There were multiple reports made in the past week of a man breaking in and stalking your whereabouts." His mustache raised as he exchanged looks with his partner.

Ethan tensed as he remained deep in thought. "I'm fine." The officers grew concerned as Ethan's phone buzzed in his pocket. "Mr. Bedford..." Ethan excused himself, walking out to the living room, hoping the distance was enough for them not to listen in as he answered the phone.

"Hello?" The voice was smooth and low. Dread filled her voice as she told Ethan. He knew it was the kind woman at the hospital. "Mr. Bedford, your mother passed last night."

His face flushed; the pit feeling came back as he didn't know how to feel. The woman he knew he hated was gone, or nearly hated, maybe? A relief, along with guilt, followed after he was sure he knew the answer. "How did she die?" A pause was at the other end of the call as she deeply sighed. "We believe her heart stopped." Ethan hung up, the feeling of knowing it was him. Always him. The image of Tatler's face ran through Ethan's mind, not realizing how hard he was clenching his phone. It looked like a second longer, it would pop.

The officers entered closely behind, as the chatter on their radios was muffled. "So the name you gave earlier, Elijah Tatler, there's no one by that name." Ethan's face never moved. Figures.

How could he be shocked after everything so far? He knew that after the police station, there was most likely nothing they could do. They never could help him. It was Ethan's doing, accepting that card. Now it was his mess to clean up.

"We can patrol and keep watch in case he comes back." Ethan turned his head down the hallway, glaring at the dolls in his bedroom.

"No thanks." The officers exchanged perplexed looks; they asked once to reassure Ethan. He slyly smiled and declined. He gently escorted them out, watching as they got into their cars and sped away. The lights slowly faded from view as he thought.

There must've been a way he was tracking him. Ethan walked to his car, scouring every inch of his car. Reaching the back trunk, he felt a small mechanical accessory loosely. He yanked as it unhitched; a small, squared black device blinked red. Ethan found it. The reason he's been watching his every move. What a pity.

∞

Chapter Twelve
I Wish You Well

Ethan stood outside the crumbling structure. The feeling of nostalgia crept in, which soon turned dark. His brief relief of sanctuary was upturned to his final dystopic stronghold. It wasn't the best place, but Tatler knew it was meaningful to him. And Ethan knew it better than anyone.

Walking around the building to the covered window. The foggy window was difficult to open, but he knew a trick. He shimmed it open and pressed his body through. In the debris of tools, a crowbar was resting. Ethan picked it up like a reward to himself for the hellish battle he was about to have.

The building reeked of rustic metal and sewage water. Ethan sat in the rubble for what felt like hours. Thoughts ran through his mind as he waited. Thoughts like whether Gregory felt this way before Tatler ended it, or if what he was doing was a mistake. Tatler was always one step ahead, and maybe this was it.

Either way, Ethan sat staring at his reflection in an old piece of sharp, crude metal. Never had he looked so worn and disheveled before.

The metal door in the distance opened; Ethan knew it was time to hide. Running behind a small crawl space and crouched, hoping Tatler wouldn't see him.

"Ethan!" The echo somber filled the stale air as Tatler ran his hand along the decayed walls.

"I know our progress wasn't this far for you to hide again. Trying to make a final stand against me now? It won't stop, Ethan. I won't stop until you're cured, because I care about you more than that unstable mother of yours." He kicked a rotted chair. "No one could save her, but you, you're special, Ethan. That's why I chose you."

Ethan grasped the crowbar tightly as Tatler unknowingly walked further from him.

Ethan took a deep breath, making sure to sound as dominant as possible. "I'm sure you know what this place is." The echoes did not allow Tatler to pinpoint the direction the voice came.

Tatler rubbed his nose and growled, "Of course. You started running away when you were twelve. This shit-shack was your second home." Tatler kicked another chair, shattering it into pieces. "I helped you! Why else would you come to me, Ethan, if not to be well?!"

Tatler slowly walked closer to the hiding space where Ethan resided. Correcting his footing for the perfect moment as Tatler yelled.

"I knew your mom was your greatest feat in your worthless life. When you were a child, she wouldn't let you grow. And when you became an adult, you held yourself back. No! No, Ethan, we exist to expand and capitalize on our limits, AND YOU'RE NOT GOING TO WASTE YOURS!" Ethan rushed at his back, missing horribly as Tatler pivoted away at the last second. Ethan swung again as Tatler smoothly dodged, grabbing Ethan by his side and slamming him into the wall. The force jerking the crowbar away from Ethan's grasp.

Tatler kicked him twice before easily lifting him up to deliver a blow to Ethan's face. The daze hit, and his world swirled as Ethan tried to grasp his bearings. His back felt as if it was on fire from the storm of kicks Tatler gave, the pain stopping him from reaching the crowbar before Tatler.

Tatler towered over Ethan with the bar in hand. "Why did you kill her? You think doing that would stop me?" Tatler gave Ethan another kick; Ethan gasped in pain, his stomach knotting. "We are bigger than you think, Ethan. And what you did, well, I don't think you were being a good boy." Tatler kicked Ethan again; he flew back into a window, the shards scattered as Ethan grabbed one as Tatler turned for a moment.

Tatler walked over to Ethan once more, pulling back his leg, preparing to swing. Ethan clung onto his leg, stabbing it three times. A blood-curdling scream came from Tatler as he collapsed. Ethan fought through the pain, crawling to the bar.

Pulling it into his hand as Tatler winced out, grasping his ankle as the red poured out rapidly.

"YOU MOTHERFUCKER!!!"

Ethan rose to his feet, beating the bar across Tatler's face. Tatler looked back at Ethan, spitting out the gore, a smile glazed his face as the bruise and blood ran over him. Ethan rose the bar up, shouting, "STOP FUCKING SMILING AT ME!" Tatler kicked Ethan, pushing himself on top of him, wrapping his hands around his throat.

Tatler spat onto Ethan, the blood causing him to blink rapidly as it blurred his vision. "You wanna know the real ending to Gregory's story?" Tatler pinned Ethan's chest down. "He asked for help just like you did, years after almost being murdered by his father's coworker. He was broken and afraid of everything! Mostly of fucking axes."

***

Gregory's body fell to the ground.

The footsteps approached slowly as if he knew he had won. Gregory was down, and no fight was to come from him. Tatler held the axe by the handle now. The butt grazed one last time across the ground.

"Gregory, Gregory. Where art thou, Gregory?" Tatler taunted him.

He, being unconscious, wasn't enough. Gregory remained lifeless as Tatler walked around him, circling his prey.

"Please don't tell me it's over that quickly." As he kicked Gregory's shoe. He jerked. He was finally coming to, not enough to process the horror standing before him. Tatler kneeled. His face spread a devilish grin.

"Too bad, I liked you." Tatler stood, lifting the axe in both hands, eyeing him down like an executioner preparing for slaughter.

Gregory looked defeated as he tried to push his eyes open. This is it. Tatler knew. His smile grew again as Gregory's tears filled his eyes.

Tatler hoisted the axe back, prepping for the crushing blow. Gregory had to fight, but what could he do? He was too weak. Tatler corrected his footing, making sure to get a solid hit.

Gregory closed his eyes, and he swung.

The clink of motion grazed past Gregory's ear as he slowly opened his eyes. The axe stuck standing into the flooring beside him.

Tatler stood above him as Gregory cried, kneeling and kissing his forehead as the sweat attached to his lips.

Gregory grabbed the axe, threatening Tatler with it. A smile washed over his face as the sight of Gregory using the weapon he couldn't stare at before.

"Imagine if you'd succumb to it like you did before." Tatler walked away into the shadows.

Gregory stared down at the axe, seeing his reflection on the blood lying on it.

***

Ethan remained pinned. Tatler pressed harder into his chest. Ethan winced as the pain grew. Tatler leaned in, his stare chilling as he spoke. "Gregory was a hard one," Tatler pressed deeper, "But not as hard as you're being, Ethan!"

Ethan's eyes widened as he gasped through every word. "You're sick."

"Am I? You completed all expectations, Ethan." Tatler gleamed; he closed his eyes and breathed deeply. Ethan took it as his signal to act. Gripping the shard of glass and running it into Tatler's stomach.

Ethan shoved him off. Tatler lay on the ground, wincing in utter silence. Ethan hovered over, punching him twice, the red glaze running out of him like water. Tatler tilted towards Ethan, muttering to himself in a final plea. Ethan dug deep in his pockets, pulling out the green mints, now crushed. Opening a few up and forcefully shoving them down Tatler's throat. The dry gulps as Tatler nearly choked.

"I- Wish··· you··· Well···Ethan."

Ethan lifted up, walking across the room, grabbing a black bag poorly hidden behind heavy pieces of glass. Pulling out the vintage camera he was bestowed earlier. Shoving it into Tatler's view before snapping a picture. The flash announced Tatler to awaken, his blue eyes piercing through the blood as he weakly reached out for Ethan.

Sirens were ringing in the distance as Ethan smiled and stared on. "Choke on it." Tatler had a look of fear as he unwillingly fell asleep.

Ethan emerged from the building, limping as the police cars pulled out front. All rushing out of their cars, one running towards Ethan. "Are you alright?" Ethan nodded as the rest rushed inside.

The exhaustion caught up with him as he fell to the ground, sighing as he looked up at the stars. The relief of a feeling he doesn't remember feeling washed over him: liberating.

"Sir?" The officer stood behind Ethan as he leaned up. Ethan remained in shock as he heard him say, "Tatler isn't there." Ethan looked in disbelief. "What?" As the officer continued, "There was DNA found, but no body. I'm sorry." Ethan looked on, more unsure than ever.

***

Ethan's body woke to the fresh air. He felt light as he lifted himself, as the morning welcomed him. He rummaged through his closet, finally pulling a clean outfit out and laying it neatly on his bed. His morning ritual began as he walked peppy towards his kitchen, on his way to his morning coffee. Breathing in the nutty aroma gave his body an exciting jolt. He needed to reassure himself for the call later today.

He knew it was a matter of time before Janice's position was open since she had her heart attack, Ethan thought. Her role was vacant, and he felt guilty, although he couldn't have directly caused whatever happened to her while she left for her office alone. Few people blamed Ethan for the angry confrontation that might have triggered it. Others assumed it was coming—karma—from her being more rotten than the dog. But he didn't want to dwell any longer. Janice would be gone, and that was that. His watch buzzed, reminding him to pull his drawer. He grabbed a small pre-opened box and pressed the patch onto his skin before stepping out.

Ethan opened the door; the air was fresh as it rushed into his nostrils. His walk was different now, more sure. His beard grew in nicely, and his shirt seemed worn but nicely fitting.

Stepping onto the concrete driveway with bare feet, he was slowly pacing himself to the mailbox. Looking around at the warming neighbors, he waved at them as they did their morning ritual chores.

Ethan pulled the door down and reached in, sorting through until a small envelope with an odd seal caught his attention.

Ethan ripped it open, curious about the contents inside. A small, perfectly folded note. Ethan undid the neatly wrapped paper, reading it as he sighed deeply. He looked on as he reflected on the impish words, knowing who it was from, knowing he was finally done with him.

Do you feel the butterflies now, Ethan?

❧

Epilogue

Her foot tapped nervously in the seat. The busy people were running to and fro to their tasks. The bell dinged twice, causing the woman to snap back to reality.

She stood, walking to the desk as the vibrant woman asked for her name.

"It'll be on the fifth floor. Then two doors to the right." The young woman nodded and headed up. Every moment in the elevator felt she needed to run, but she knew it was a chance to get better, and this was a perfect opportunity.

The doors dinged before opening. The floor was quiet. Her attention was immediately drawn to the tarp-covered room. Everything was coated from the ceiling to the floor. And it hadn't looked like it needed any renovating. She could tell there was equipment underneath, and why not take it out instead of having it stay in? Although it wasn't her business, and she didn't want to have her body retreat to the wild thoughts surrounded by that tarp-covered room, for the triggers would build. Maybe they're painting. The second door was in view now. She knocked lightly and opened the door slowly.

Tatler sat in the chair at the corner of the room, completely fresh as if all the grotesque things months before had never occurred. He lightly traced the notes in his lap as she approached.

"Come in." His deceivingly warming voice coaxed the room as she sat in the lush couch across from him.

Tightly she sat, shelled into the couch. He lifted his head slowly. "So what brings you in today?"

Unbeknownst to her, he would help her beat the butterflies.